SEASONALITY

Wiley Trading Advantage Series

SEASONALITY

Systems, Strategies, and Signals

JAKE BERNSTEIN

JOHN WILEY & SONS, INC.

New York • Chichester • Weinheim • Brisbane • Singapore • Toronto

This book is printed on acid-free paper.⊗

This publication is designed to provide accurate and authoritative information in regard to the subject matter covered. It is sold with the understanding that the publisher is not engaged in rendering legal, accounting, or other professional services. If legal advice or other expert assistance is required, the services of a competent professional person should be sought.

Library of Congress Cataloging-in-Publication Data:

Bernstein, Jacob, 1946–
    Seasonality: systems, strategies, and signals. / Jake Bernstein.
        p.   cm.—(Wiley trading advantage series)
    Includes index.
    ISBN 0-471-16811-4 (alk. paper)
    1. Stocks—Prices.   2. Seasonal variations (Economics).   I. Title.
    II. Series.
    HG4636,B493   1998
    332.63′222—dc21   97-38741

Printed in the United States of America

10 9 8 7 6 5 4 3 2 1

PREFACE

Traders have given considerable attention to the role of supply, demand, earnings, underlying economic conditions, interest rates, inflation trends, money supply, and a host of other variables regarding the prices of stocks and commodities, but they have consistently and persistently ignored the importance of seasonality. Although traders, investors, and analysts may have their private reasons for ignoring seasonal factors and forces as significant to market trends, the primary reason, I believe, is their ignorance. The simple fact is that most traders and market analysts are not aware of the impact that seasonal price tendencies can have on trends in stock and commodity prices.

Another reason for the general lack of interest in seasonality is that many traders confuse seasonality with weather, often equating the two. This error leads them to the wrong conclusion that a market such as the Swiss franc cannot exhibit a seasonal pattern because it cannot be affected by weather. Based on my extensive seasonal research since the early 1970s, such a conclusion is incorrect; it also reveals ignorance and closed-mindedness. Traders who seek success would do well to heed the lessons of seasonality.

In addition to my own research, a number of respected market analysts and economic researchers have helped further the cause of seasonality, including MBH Commodity Advisors, Inc. (Winnetka, Ill.), and Commodity Research Bureau (Chicago). The pioneering work of the

Foundation for the Study of Cycles (Wayne, Pa.) and the seasonally oriented findings of W. D. Gann, Art Merrill, Burton Pugh, Samuel Benner, and Yale Hirsch have been significant but have barely scratched the surface of what may yet be achieved by detailed statistical analysis of seasonal price trends. Paradoxically, traders and investors strive relentlessly to find systems, methods, indicators, techniques, schemes and approaches that yield consistent profits with limited or reasonable risk, yet they tend to ignore those methods that are among the most effective and logical. Today, seasonality in stock and commodity prices remains one of the best-kept market secrets. Perhaps the concepts and methods explained in this book will help to increase the awareness and use of seasonal concepts.

IS COMPLICATED BETTER THAN SIMPLE?

We live in an age of fascination with the complex. We have been mentally and behaviorally conditioned to place great value on what is difficult to understand and achieve, and to look askance at that which is logical, readily understandable, or otherwise uncomplicated. The age of elementary Cartesian logic and empiricism, which formed the cornerstones of scientific advances, has been lost to the lure of fuzzy logic and artificial intelligence. I have no argument with the need for more advanced forms of intellectual and scientific reasoning, but we must also remember that many of the basics still apply.

Of all the concepts that a futures trader can learn, one of the simplest is seasonality. In fact, of all the logical concepts that a futures trader can learn, the most basic, the most readily understandable, and the most easily applied is seasonality. Yet many traders seem to prefer to wallow in a sea of complexities. They struggle with subjective concepts and work laboriously for hours on end, analyzing markets with numerous indicators, rather than complete their arduous task by using time-tested and reliable concepts.

Seasonality may not be the Holy Grail of futures trading; nevertheless, the use of seasonal concepts and methods in futures trading can do the following:

- Lead to objective decisions based on a logical and operational methodology.

- Facilitate the development of a solid, analytical decision-making framework.
- Provide a backdrop of probable market trends in most time frames and in most markets.
- Improve your odds of success as a trader by focusing on historically valid patterns and methodologies.
- Assist in the selection of historically valid seasonal spread trends.
- Provide historically valid input for use as an adjunct to other analytical methods and timing indicators.

That is what the use of seasonal concepts in futures trading *can* do for you. Here is what the use of seasonal concepts *cannot* do for you:

- Be the ultimate, fail-safe method to achieving vast wealth.
- Give you perfect market timing.
- Be correct all the time.
- Eliminate the risk of futures trading.
- Give you deep insights as to the meaning of market trends or their causes.

The following are my primary goals in publishing this book:

- *To increase public awareness of seasonality.* This is my most ambitious goal. For too many years, too few traders have been aware of how reliable seasonals have been in virtually all markets. My intent is not only to make the major seasonals known to all readers, but also to point out their relative accuracy (or lack thereof) and to highlight the ideal time frames of high probability up-and-down moves in the various markets as well as in spreads. I illustrate the history and efficacy of seasonality in daily, weekly, and monthly time frames and in an objective and historically valid fashion so as to dispel any ideas that seasonal patterns are merely random events or artifacts of historical data.
- *To provide a logical and effective trading framework for the use of seasonals.* I provide objective and logical seasonal methods that range from market analysis to precise seasonal trade implementation complete with risk management. Traders who are

interested in progressing beyond the methods outlined in this book will be able to do so readily, using any of several timing methods that I suggest.

- *To emphasize the validity of seasonality as a long-term as well as a short-term method.* The fact that seasonality exists in all time frames is a strong testimonial to its validity as an underlying fact of market life. This book provides numerous examples of seasonality in different time frames and suggests various ways to use the seasonal time frames.

- *To balance facts and underlying causes.* Traders can profit in several ways by using technical market methods. They can impose their own framework on the markets, trading within the dictates of their parameters, or they can attempt to trade within parameters that are a function of underlying market behavior. This duality is similar to the analogy in medicine between the treatment of symptoms and the treatment of underlying causes. Both methods can be effective; both can be ineffective. The purist would argue that understanding underlying causes is the only valid approach, since it deals in reality. Technicians would argue that merely understanding the "why" of things does not guarantee profitable timing or trading, and they would argue as well that timing is more important than understanding.

   In fact, seasonality combines some of the best features of both approaches. On the one hand, it is both the explanation of the fact and the fact at the same time. Seasonality has a basis in fact, not in theory. In other words, most of the time we know what causes a seasonal move to occur. In addition, we know how often seasonal moves have occurred. Although I do not attempt to predict the future use of seasonality, I do believe that seasonals that have shown a particular tendency for many years are likely to continue that tendency. Hence, a seasonal is a technical fact as well as a fundamental condition. If this distinction is unclear to you now, I assure you that it will become abundantly clear as you read this book.

- *To demonstrate that seasonality has a place in all trading systems.* Filtering a trading system by including major seasonal moves as an input can substantially improve overall performance. This is not to say that the marriage between seasonals and technicals will always be effective. Sometimes, of course, seasonals are either wrong or have shifted in their timing, and the sad but true fact is that during such times, seasonals lose money. There is no avoiding the market reality that seasonality is not perfect; nevertheless, it can be a great asset.

A CAVEAT

I assume that readers are well acquainted with the risk of loss in futures trading and that they have sufficient knowledge, intelligence, and risk capital to trade the markets and understand the inherent risks. Yet by decree of the regulatory agencies that oversee the futures markets, as well as those of us who write about the markets, I am required to restate the caveat. Please consider this warning to be my due diligence in fulfilling the legal mandate to forewarn you of the risks.

JAKE BERNSTEIN

Northbrook, Illinois
February 1998

CONTENTS

APPENDIX D

APPENDIX E

INDEX   211

SEASONALITY

SEASONALITY

1

SEASONALITY, PRICE HISTORY, AND HUMANKIND

THE AGE-OLD QUEST

For thousands of years, people have been fascinated with the prospect of someday controlling nature. This hope continues to flourish to this day, and technological advances in weather forecasting have kept the dream alive. Advances in genetic engineering as well as in weather forecasting have fueled the flames of control. The ability to control nature, which in fact controls us, has vast ramifications in virtually every area of life: social, political, economic, and agricultural. Nevertheless, it is unlikely that we will ever be able to control or predict nature fully.

Arguably, the desire to control nature originated in the human quest for survival. Inasmuch as nourishment and shelter are two of the most basic human needs, issues relating to their fulfillment have always been central considerations in human life. The utopian view of an environment constantly stable and perfectly engineered to maximize comfort and the growth of crops and livestock will not likely be achieved in our lifetime, but the hope is nonetheless undiminished.

Imagine an environment perfectly suited to the most efficient production of crops and livestock. Imagine as well a world tailored to optimum conditions for recreation. In such a perfectly engineered world,

1

humans would be free to follow their pursuits without concern about the limitations of weather. The most significant benefits of weather control, of course, would be those that would ultimately help feed all the peoples in the world. Starvation would disappear (provided the politics of food distribution did not interfere with the increased production of crops and animals).

POSSIBILITIES, UNDERSTANDINGS, AND POTENTIAL

The possibilities of what might be achieved in such a state are vast. What would our priorities be: to feed the starving, or to achieve the greatest profit? Would the control of weather become a political tool for ruthless rulers? Would it become the basis for still more political conflict? It is unlikely that we will ever know the answers to these questions in the course of our lifetime. Clearly, the control of nature is a task so immense, a goal so lofty and ambitious, that in spite of our advanced and steadily growing technological skills, it is most likely unattainable in the foreseeable future. I am not saying that certain limited aspects of our environment are beyond control, nor am I saying that minor environmental changes cannot be achieved in the near future. I am, however, expressing doubt about the extent to which such control is attainable.

Of course, the term *control* as applied to virtually any endeavor nowadays is politically incorrect. A necessary aspect of control is responsibility. If control of the weather ever becomes a reality, it will bring with it a plethora of issues—ethical, moral, legal, and social—that will require resolution. Indeed all progress has negative and regressive aspects as well as positive ones.

Perhaps the next best thing to control is understanding. In understanding the cause-and-effect relationships of a situation, it is often possible to predict, within reasonable limits, when changes will occur. This view is a mechanistic or empirical one, which assumes that cause and effect actually do exist. There is a considerable body of philosophical thought that calls into serious question the value of and/or the existence of cause and effect. These are, however, beyond the scope of my discussion and analysis in this book.

The skill to predict when environmental change is most likely to occur adds immeasurably to the repertoire of our preparedness to cope with nature's changes. Therefore, advance knowledge of nature's possible changes can lead to action, and positive action ultimately leads to survival and growth. However, positive action cannot proceed without an understanding of how the forces of weather operate to bring about change. In this respect, the ability to forecast weather patterns correctly is a function of the ability to understand the dynamics and scientific basis of weather.

The ability to forecast weather—to understand the seasonal changes in nature and prepare for these events—is vital to human survival. Consider the catastrophic events that have occurred as a result of our inability to forecast and prepare for cataclysmic changes in weather. Unexpected twisters, storms, hurricanes, and floods have taken a vast toll through the centuries. Immense loss of life, crops, livestock, shelter, and natural resources could have been avoided or significantly reduced had we been able to predict such catastrophes.

The Cyclical Nature of Weather Patterns

Research has shown that weather patterns tend to repeat themselves, often following cycles that can be up to hundreds of years in length.[1] The writings, research, and teachings of Leonard W. Wing are only one small aspect of the effort made in this direction. Wing discovered many critical relationships in weather and temperature patterns, yet his work is still relatively unknown. There is a growing body of evidence to suggest that the ultimate cause of weather patterns is related to the cycles in sunspot numbers. The Foundation for the Study of Cycles (in Wayne, Pennsylvania) has examined sunspot cycles extensively and has documented their existence, as well as their predictability and correlation with weather patterns on earth.[2]

Weather Patterns and Human Emotion

The Russian professor S. L. Tchijevsky was specific in his assertion that humanity is a slave to the seasons. In 1926, he wrote:

---

[1] E. R. Dewey, *Cycles—Selected Writings* (Pittsburgh: Foundation for the Study of Cycles, 1970), pp. 761–765.

[2] Ibid., pp. 750–759.

In the middle points of the cycle, the mass activity of all humanity, assuming the presence in human societies of economical, political or military exciting factors, reaches the maximum tension, manifesting itself in psychomotoric pandemics, revolutions, insurrections, expeditions, migrations, etc.—thus creating new formations in the existing separate states and new historical epochs in the life of humanity. It is accompanied by an integration of the masses, a full expression of their activity and a form of government consisting of a majority.

In the extreme points of the cycle's course, the tension of the all human military-political activity falls to the minimum, giving way to creative activity and is accompanied by a general decrease of military or political enthusiasm, by peace and peaceful relations, science and art, with a pronounced tendency towards absolutism in the governing powers and a disintegration of the masses.[3]

W. D. Gann: High and Low Seasonality in the Stock Market and Soybean Prices

The work of W. D. Gann, the legendary stock and commodity trader, was quite clear in its tenets regarding seasonality in the stock and commodity markets. In *How to Make Profits in Commodities,* Garr noted the seasonal pattern of soybean prices from 1913 to 1941, as follows:

Soy Beans—Months When the Most High and Low Prices Have Been Reached

This covers the period from 1913 to 1941, or 28 years.

During this period:

January	High 4 times	Low 7 times
February	High 3 times	Low 7 times
March	High 2 times	No Lows
April	High 1 time	No Lows
May	High 3 times	No Lows
June	High 3 times	No Lows
July	High 3 times	Low 2 times

[3]S. L. Horner, "Tchijevsky's Index of Mass Human Excitability 500 B.C.–A.D. 1922," *Journal of Cycle Research,* vol. 9, no. 1, January 1960, p. 23.

August	High 1 time	Low 2 times
September	High 1 time	Low 1 time
October	High 3 times	Low 11 times
November	High 1 time	Low 5 times
December	High 2 times	Low 5 times

From the above you can see that most *Highs* have been reached in January, the month when seasonal *Lows* are usually reached in Corn and Wheat. Soy Beans have made, *High* 3 times during May, June and July and 3 times during October and 3 times in February. The months when the least number of *Highs* have been made are April, August and September; also November. In each of these months only one *High* has been reached during the 28-year period. From this record you would expect seasonal *Highs* in January and February at certain times when the market was running opposite the seasonal trend, then you would watch the *Highs* in May, June and July. And, if the crops were very short and the market running against seasonal trend, you would expect *Highs* in October.[4]

Furthermore, Gann states: "Because stocks run according to seasonal changes and make extreme highs in certain months . . . it is important to go over past records . . . of these important moves."[5]

Figure 1-1 shows the monthly cash soybean seasonal trend from 1930 through 1996. Clearly the chart agrees with Gann's findings. Seasonal grain and soybean prices have been highly reliable.

That there are seasonal price patterns in stock and commodity prices is the primary subject of this book, yet my ideas regarding seasonal fluctuations in the markets are not new. What may be unique or relatively new is my methodology and point of view that seasonality in the markets is not always a function of weather or the seasons. Rather, seasonality exists in virtually all stock and commodity markets, as well as in virtually all aspects of economic data, and its existence can be demonstrated logically, empirically, and statistically. Although I state my case with regard to the causal factors of seasonal price movements in the markets, I am not a proponent of discovering underlying causes.

[4]W. D. Gann, *How to Make Profits in Commodities* (Pomeroy, Wash.: Lambert-Gann, 1942), p. 127.
[5]Ibid., p. 82.

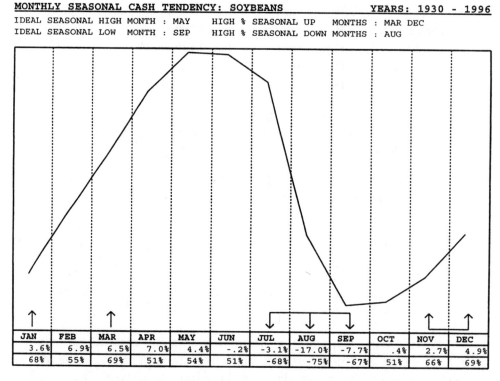

MONTHLY SEASONAL CASH TENDENCY: SOYBEANS   YEARS: 1930 - 1996

IDEAL SEASONAL HIGH MONTH : MAY   HIGH % SEASONAL UP   MONTHS : MAR DEC
IDEAL SEASONAL LOW MONTH : SEP   HIGH % SEASONAL DOWN MONTHS : AUG

JAN	FEB	MAR	APR	MAY	JUN	JUL	AUG	SEP	OCT	NOV	DEC
3.6%	6.9%	6.5%	7.0%	4.4%	-.2%	-3.1%	-17.0%	-7.7%	.4%	2.7%	4.9%
68%	55%	69%	51%	54%	51%	-68%	-75%	-67%	51%	66%	69%

Figure 1-1   Yearly high and low counts of soybeans by month; 1930–1996. In this and similar charts, the line plot shows the average seasonal trend and the arrows indicate a high probability of up and down moves. At the bottom of the chart, the first row of percentages are the average percent change for the month; the second row shows the percentage of time the average price has moved up or down for the month. (Copyright © 1997 by MBH Commodity Advisors, Inc.)

An up movement in the Swiss franc caused by recurrent banking activity at given times of the year is no less significant than is an up movement in orange juice prices resulting from cold weather in January. To the speculator, underlying causes are of little value unless he or she can know the underlying causes well in advance of their occurrence. When I awake in the morning and see the sun, I spend little, if any, time wondering why the sun rises. When I awake in the morning and fail to see the sun under its cover of dark clouds, I do not ask why the sun fails to shine or why the clouds threaten rain. I accept these events as the ways of nature and the world.

But stock and commodity traders view events, as well as cause and effect, from a different perspective. All too often they seek to understand the "why and wherefore" of market movements—a natural desire, particularly when it relates to risking one's hard-earned money on trading or investing. Therefore, I attempt to answer some of the why and wherefore questions about seasonality, although I do not spend much time or space in doing so. Readers who wish to delve deeper into the cause-and-effect aspects of seasonality may do so at their leisure. (If it can assist them in finding meaningful or profitable strategies for seasonal trading, I encourage such explorations.)

SEASONALS AND STRATEGIC VALUE

The issue of greatest importance regarding seasonality is that its effects are not only environmental and agricultural, but economic as well. For example, the United States at its core is an agrarian economy that still ranks as the top supplier of foodstuffs to the world. Most Third World countries are almost exclusively agrarian. All nations are dependent on a constant source of nourishment for their survival. Therefore, climatological disruptions and anomalies have an almost immediate economic effect on a global level. Food that is lost through severe weather must be replaced, or consumption must decline. It can be replaced only by purchase or barter. In this way, weather directly affects the economy of any nation that suffers crop or livestock damage.

Even the nations of the former Soviet Union, in spite of their vast land mass and immense resources of petroleum and gold, have had to turn to the world markets when they suffer agricultural shortfalls resulting from disruptions in weather. In order to purchase their required allotment of foodstuffs, nations must generate cash or loans, by either cutting back on spending or increasing production in areas other than agriculture (e.g., sell petroleum or sell gold), which affects price trends in these markets. Hence, the effects of weather can be far reaching. But it must be emphasized that weather is only one cause of seasonal price movement.

An Example: Petroleum Price Trends

During the 1970s and 1980s, the use of petroleum as a significant strategic weapon became painfully evident. Middle Eastern countries that control vast petroleum resources threatened embargo and instituted price fixing in conjunction with other petroleum-producing countries through the Organization of Petroleum Exporting Countries (OPEC). The effects of such control were felt throughout the world as petroleum prices gyrated wildly during that time.

The importance of petroleum was accentuated during the Gulf War, when prices shot up dramatically. Figure 1-2 shows the price trend in fuel oil from 1939 through 1997. That prices since the 1970s have precipitously increased is clear. This has had an effect on agriculture, inflation, precious metals, currencies, and political events. Although most traders and investors saw the Gulf War as a relatively random event, the fact is that within the history of petroleum prices, there have been a number of reliable and repetitive patterns that ap-

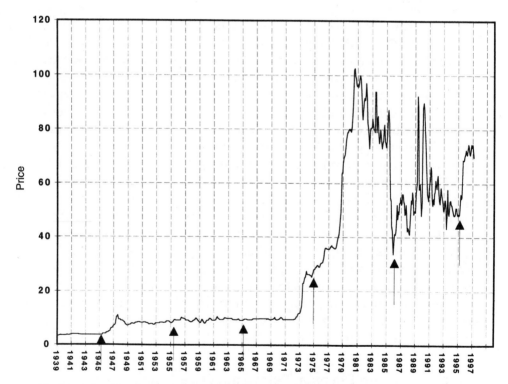

Figure 1-2   The approximate 10-11 cycle in lows in fuel oil prices, 1939–1997. The arrows point out the 10-year cycles. (Copyright © 1997 by MBH Commodity Advisors, Inc.)

pear to have had consistency regardless of international events. The major pattern of importance is a 10-year cycle, shown by the arrows in Figure 1-2. This OPEC example illustrates one of the most serious of the far-reaching consequences that may occur when a nation or group of nations seeks to control strategic commodities.

During the same period of time, the United States tried to control the availability of various goods (primarily high technology) sold to nations not having favored status. These controls were unsuccessful, since there was no organized effort on the part of other producing nations to cooperate in the embargo. Concomitantly, voices were raised in support of a grain embargo originally instituted against Poland by President Jimmy Carter for alleged human rights violations. Although the embargo had virtually no effect other than to lower U.S. grain prices, the mere effort to apply political pressure using agricultural commodities illustrates the increasing significance of agricultural goods in today's world.

Although I make no judgments about such methods of international political and price control, it is my firm belief that the greatest strategic weapon is food, not, as some would have us believe, petroleum. Food can be produced without petroleum and, in fact, without virtually any other source of power except human energy. Nations that have no agricultural resources are especially vulnerable to agricultural embargoes, particularly if an organized international cartel is supporting the embargo. Nevertheless, all efforts to use agricultural production as a strategic weapon remain dependent on the availability of this weapon. The availability of food is directly a function of seasonal factors. Without the cooperation of nature, this greatest strategic weapon can be rendered useless. Regardless of how powerful a nation may be by virtue of its petroleum, its gold, or its agricultural resources, it is the weather that ultimately determines the distribution, storage, and allocation of these resources.

Even the OPEC nations are limited in their control of petroleum prices by environmental factors. Consider fuel oil prices during late 1983 and early 1984. Toward the end of 1983, oil was in plentiful supply. Reserves in the United States were at their highest level in several years, and prices had declined. Many experts thought that the downturn would continue due to an economic slowdown and increased petroleum production. Then came the weather, which rendered the experts wrong. Over the course of several weeks, as temperatures plunged in Europe and the United States, heating oil prices surged upward.

That the weather is a causative agent in some price movements is fairly obvious to even the most casual observer; nevertheless, there are many seasonal price movements over the course of a year for which there appear to be no logical rhyme or reason. This may well seem to be the case, but the fact is that if we take time to search for the causes, we will find them. I provide specific illustrations as we progress through the seasonal concepts and methods explained in this book.

MORE PRICE PATTERNS: RECENT FINDING ON CYCLES IN DROUGHTS AND FLOODS

Recent research has verified the importance of weather cycles regarding drought and flood. In the March 1985 issue of *Cycles,* John Burns, executive director of the Foundation for the Study of Cycles, which publishes *Cycles,* referred to G. Currie, who has researched a host of cyclic patterns in air temperature, sea level, flood, droughts, and the rate of the earth's rotation and has published numerous studies showing an almost incredible periodic fluctuation in such patterns. Burns notes that Currie's research provides new insights into the mechanism and action of cycles. Furthermore, our understanding of cycles based on Currie's work can help the world's agricultural producers plan better, thereby avoiding much of the starvation that has been experienced, particularly in recent years. On a more pragmatic level, an understanding of these cycles for producers provides one of the strongest planning tools ever available. Here is what Burns wrote:

> Specifically I want to tell you of the study by Robert G. Currie on "Periodic (18.6-year) and Cyclic (11-year) Induced Drought and Flood in Western North America." This paper also reviews his earlier work, which encompasses cyclic studies on such things as air temperature, sea level, and rate of the earth's rotation, floods and droughts. In these time series, he has described 18.7-year cycles and/or 11-year cycles. As you probably recognize, the 18.6-year cycle corresponds to the nodal cycle of the moon found in the ties and the 11-year cycle corresponds to the sunspot cycle.
>
> Currie claims that the implications for agriculture and the world's food supply are sufficient that even now our understanding of cyclical patterns can be used to avoid much starvation. Thus he points to 1991.9, as the time to prepare for when the next nodal

pattern (18.6-year) is likely (p = .092) to result in drought in the continental interior of North America. This drought would be similar to other "nodal droughts" of this century that corresponded to the ideal times of 1917.5, 1936.1, 1954.7 and 1973.3, i.e., previous maxim in the 18.6-year tidal cycle.

The 11-year cyclic pattern is not as influential on drought and floods as the 18.6-year cycle. Currie finds, however, that there is a "solar cycle modulation" of the previously discussed nodal pattern. Thus, 1843.0, 1861.6 and 1936.1 were times when the maxims in solar and nodal drought were aligned within 1 year. This relationship may provide an explanation for the severity of the Dust Bowl.

Even more amazing to me is the finding that the phase relationships were found to vary geographically. For example, maxima in the lunar nodal 18.6-year drought in Western Canada were out of phase, by about 9 years with those in the Western United States and Northern Mexico during the past two centuries. It will be interesting to eventually learn the cause of this geographic effect.

The importance of cycle research can hardly be overestimated. Now we are beginning to see the real strength of interdisciplinary cycle studies and how this knowledge is vital to the whole world inasmuch as we are all dependent on the U.S. crop production.[6]

ENVIRONMENTAL CONCERNS AND SEASONALITY

Weather is thus more than just the right seasons coming at the right time; it is the greatest single expression of nature's power over humanity and, conversely, of our dependence on its effects. Is it any wonder that the dreams and visions of men and women have so long been preoccupied by their desire to control the seasons? Yet there is more to the "control of nature" than meets the eye. Our ecosystem represents an entity in virtually perfect balance. It is a system that has evolved through millions of years of development, and it maintains its internal balance exceptionally well. Only recently have environmentalists discovered the disruptive effects of tampering with nature's ways. One small attempt to control the apparently most minor segment of the natural balance can have far-reaching consequences in the system itself.

[6]J. T. Burns, "Letter from the Director," *Cycles*, vol. 36, no. 2, pp. 27–28.

The abundance or paucity of certain life-forms—bacteria, reptile, insect, or mammal—can have a chain-reaction effect on thousands of other life-forms in the biological chain. But because of the vast size and global interaction of nature's machinery, such changes frequently take many years before humans directly experience their effects. A large machine takes much time and energy to move; once in motion, however, it is difficult to stop. Recent concerns about such matters as the greenhouse effect have prompted speculation that a general warming trend in the earth's environment may significantly affect weather patterns, and thereby agricultural production, throughout the world.

In 1984, National Educational Television produced a series of reports highlighting this subject. It noted the serious nature of such potential changes—for example:

NARRATOR: But specific regional climate change is among the most speculative of modeling predictions. But some scenarios have been.

Drought-stricken northeast Africa, for example, could have an increase in rain and possibly become a grain producer.

In India, the chance of more rain might produce an extra crop of rice.

The United Kingdom could have a significant temperature rise with changes in rainfall. It might be like the Middle Ages again when vineyards flourished here.

In the Central Plains of Russia, increased temperatures might lengthen the growing season by two weeks or so, promising increasing yields—if the water could be found.

And more CO_2 could make plants grow faster everywhere. In this same scenario, the modelers' prediction is very different for central North America.

This is the principal grain-exporting region of the world. Rich soils, together with warm summers and generous rainfall, have made it known as the "breadbasket of the world." Half the world's corn is grown here.

The grain belt, which includes Indiana, Illinois, Wisconsin and Iowa, and stretches from Texas in the south to the Dakotas in the north and on into Canada, produces 200 of the world's grains.

The North American crop totals a quarter-billion tons each year. And one-third of that is exported.

Could a few degrees warming threaten this harvest?

DR. STEPHEN SCHNEIDER: A few degrees warming may not seem like much, but it can have important influences anyway. The way people feel climate is more through the extremes than through the average.

For example in 1983, we know there was an extended heat wave in the Midwest and in the southeast which hurt elderly, who were not in air conditioned rooms, and reduced corn yields considerably.

NARRATOR: The prospect of higher temperatures and less rain could be serious for this region.

DANNY STEPHENS: Well, the yield reduction may be 50 percent or so—just depends on how much water you get. It takes a lot of water.[7]

There have been countless examples of environmental changes throughout recorded history. Notwithstanding some of the more obvious effects of weather such as Hitler's major defeats during an excessively cold winter on the Soviet front, the defeat of Napoleon of Waterloo, and the United States' loss of the war in the jungles of Vietnam, many additional consequences of environmental extremes go unnoticed at first but reach serious proportions in the long run.

PREDICTING SEASONALITY

I have taken the long way of making my point to illustrate the immense value of understanding seasonality. Although I am not taking a historically deterministic point of view relative to seasonality, I believe nevertheless that the seasonal forces and their related effects rank among the most significant aspects of historical cause and effect. Inasmuch as most of humans' impact on weather has been primarily negative (due to such things as atomic testing, defoliation, and air pol-

[7]"The Climate Crisis," *Nova*, no. 1019 (Boston: WGBH, 1984), p. 15.

lution), it is reasonable to assume that it will take many years of concerted effort to control weather in a positive fashion. In fact, it will likely take many years and billions of dollars to undo the damage that has already been done.

Since control of nature is a goal of limited probability for the foreseeable future, another goal thereby attains primary importance: prediction. If we cannot control, then we must seek to predict, through study and understanding. In order to study effectively, we must assess pertinent historical factors in all areas of seasonality and weather cycles. Inasmuch as seasonality has its primary effects on agriculture, those parties directly affected by such seasonal forces would do well to familiarize themselves with seasonal price patterns, which occur as a direct or indirect function of the seasons themselves.

Seasonals in Virtually All Markets

For many years, it was believed that only agricultural commodity prices are directly affected by seasonal factors. Such an assumption was certainly justified based on what was obvious to producers and consumers. Closer study, however, has revealed that virtually all markets exhibit seasonal price fluctuations. The copper market, for example, tends to be highly seasonal, although weather itself may not account directly for its price fluctuations.

One aspect of copper seasonality involves the amount of new construction, both in process and in the planning stage. Demand for copper is a result of builders' needs in home construction for plumbing, electrical wire, and metal alloys. Certainly weather considerations in construction expenditures play an important role in only some geographic areas; however, the degree of demand affected is sufficiently large to make its effects known in the price equation regardless of weather. Other fundamental seasonal factors have also been observed in interest rates, precious metals, currencies, lumber prices, and security prices. Indeed, virtually all commodities are affected in some way by seasonal forces regardless of weather.

Seasonal cycles are often highly regular and sufficiently predictable to allow producers and consumers planning time in expectation of, and in preparation for, such changes. Such seasonal variations as residential construction contracts are discounted and to some extent may

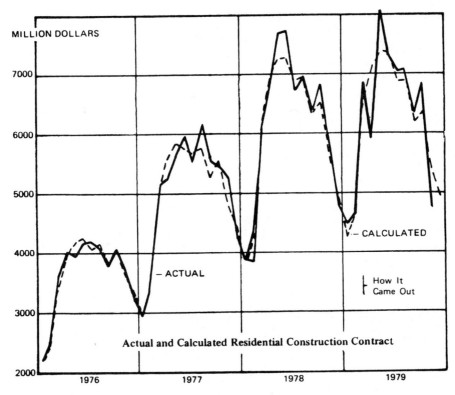

Figure 1-3 Seasonal cycle in residential construction contracts. (From *Catalogue of Cycles,* Wayne, Pa.: Foundation for the Study of Cycles, 1982.)

become self-fulfilling prophecies. The seasonal cycle in construction contracts, shown over a four-year period in Figure 1-3, is not only highly regular but highly predictable too. Figures 1-4, 1-5, and 1-6 show seasonal price tendencies as well in the copper, Swiss franc, and T-bond yields.

A Working Definition of Seasonality

Let us take a step back and state a working definition of seasonality: The term *seasonality* refers to the intrayear fluctuations of a given variable or indicator to the extent that such fluctuation is reasonably

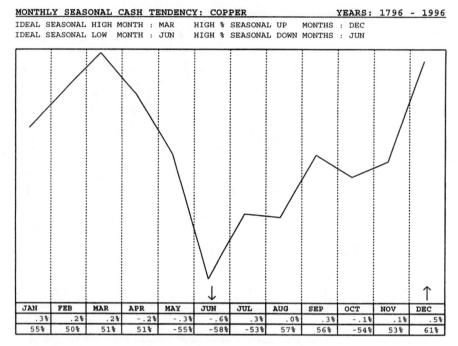

Figure 1-4   Monthly seasonal pattern in cash copper prices, 1796–1996. (Copyright © 1997 by MBH Commodity Advisors, Inc.)

regular and sufficiently predictable. The term seasonality does not necessarily suggest that weather is the only cause of seasonality. Such effect may be either indirect or entirely unobservable. Any variable that demonstrates a fairly predictable and regular intrayear pattern of fluctuation is said to exhibit a seasonal tendency.

The important aspect of this definition is the distinction between season per se and seasonality. *Season* refers to the weather itself and its annual changes; *seasonality* includes intrayear price changes that are not necessarily limited to direct or observable weather-related effects. Perhaps research may uncover the causes of seasonal fluctuation in markets not directly affected by weather. For example, it may be that the direct effect of weather is on humans, and humans in turn are influenced by weather to act in certain ways. One of these ways may be economic in its ramifications.

MONTHLY SEASONAL CASH TENDENCY: SWISSFR   YEARS: 1913 - 1996

IDEAL SEASONAL HIGH MONTH : DEC   HIGH % SEASONAL UP   MONTHS : JUN
IDEAL SEASONAL LOW MONTH : MAR   HIGH % SEASONAL DOWN MONTHS : JAN

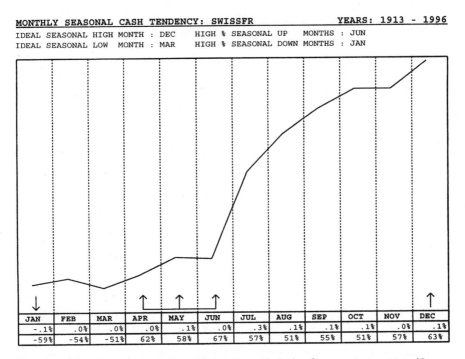

JAN	FEB	MAR	APR	MAY	JUN	JUL	AUG	SEP	OCT	NOV	DEC
-.1%	.0%	.0%	.0%	.1%	.0%	.3%	.1%	.1%	.1%	.0%	.1%
-59%	-54%	-51%	62%	58%	67%	57%	51%	55%	51%	57%	63%

Figure 1-5 Monthly seasonal pattern in cash Swiss franc, 1913–1996. (Copyright © 1997 by MBH Commodity Advisors, Inc.)

Consider the seasonal fluctuation of frozen pork belly prices. You might assume that the frozen pork belly market would not be affected by weather, since the product (bacon) is frozen and can be stored for fairly long periods of time. During times of oversupply, pigs may be slaughtered, the midsection removed, and the product frozen and stored for later sale and consumption. Because of the ability to process meat in this fashion, it would seem that the effect of weather would be a minor consideration in the price structure of bacon. In fact, this is not the case. The demand for bacon increases during the summer months, causing prices to peak in the summer months, falling through the winter months as consumption declines. I am certain that with a good amount of study, fundamental explanations could be advanced to clarify the cause of this pattern. Explanations, however, are not the stuff of which profits are made, by either the investor or the agricultural pro-

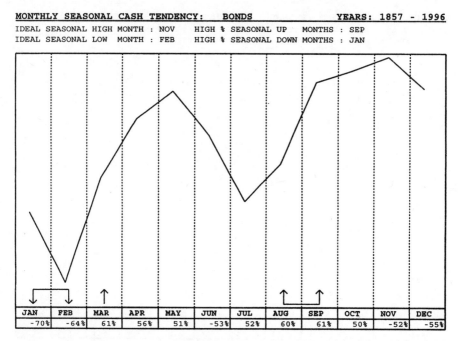

Figure 1-6   Monthly seasonal pattern in T-bond yields, 1857–1996. (Copyright ©
1997 by MBH Commodity Advisors, Inc.)

ducer. It is one thing to know why something happens; it is yet a significantly more important thing to know that something happens on a
cyclical basis.

The analyses and methods discussed in this book will provide you
with guidelines for dealing with the major issues in seasonal price
behavior.

2

AN OVERVIEW OF SEASONAL RESEARCH

Since 1970, the development of seasonal concepts and methods has accelerated rapidly, and so have their acceptance by the futures trading community. In fact, the popularity of seasonal methods has grown substantially since the late 1980s. Today, seasonality is an acceptable and valuable methodology in the repertoire of many futures traders and analysts. Nevertheless, its role as an important price-related variable is still not fully acknowledged.

In the 1950s and 1960s, many traders agreed that seasonal behavior is an observable entity in the futures markets, but they were generally unaware of the precise nature of seasonal patterns on a weekly, monthly, or even daily basis. The task of isolating seasonal price patterns from a vast database of historical prices was a laborious undertaking before the development of computers. Furthermore, traders lacked the methodology to implement seasonal trades effectively once they had been isolated.

In the 1960s and early 1970s, the shell egg futures market at the Chicago Mercantile Exchange was perhaps the best-known "seasonal market." Egg production is directly influenced by the weather conditions in which laying hens are raised. Within an optimum temperature range, egg production is at its maximum. Below a given temperature and above a given temperature, egg production declines. Under conditions of extreme heat, chickens die at a rapid rate. During the summer months, egg futures prices are prone to rally, often strongly, in response to increased temperatures. The seasonal tendency in shell egg futures prices can be observed in Figure 2-1, a weekly price chart that shows the behavior of shell egg futures prices from 1968 through 1978. I have marked the period of seasonal price increases with arrows. As you can see, the price rallies were very regular and sometimes very large. The magnitude of the rallies was closely correlated with the magnitude of temperatures.

Shell egg futures exhibited a reliable seasonal pattern for many years, with the start or continuation of a nice rally in June and July every year. This pattern ended when air-conditioned hen houses were introduced to combat the effects of excessive heat on egg products.

Ultimately the egg futures market ceased to be a viable trading entity, and trading volume declined to virtually nil. The primary reason for this decline was the introduction of air-conditioned hen houses, which neutralized the role of temperature as a causative factor in egg price movement since excessive heat was no longer a factor in reducing egg production. I mention the egg futures market because many of today's traders were introduced to the vital role of seasonality in the futures markets by observing the often severe effect of weather patterns on the price of eggs.

Seasonality was also known to play a role in many other futures markets. Veteran grain and livestock traders, for example, have long been familiar with the effect of weather on prices. The more obvious effects—for example, the impact of excessive moisture or temperature on crops—had been known for many years. Nevertheless, few recognized the highly repetitive role of more subtle seasonal patterns, such as those that were not a direct function of weather but rather a result of marketing patterns, interest rate trends, consumption patterns, or underlying economic factors.

As more traders and market analysts accepted the concept of seasonality, the number of studies and trading methods based on seasonals increased. Today virtually all futures traders are familiar with seasonal patterns, not only in the agricultural commodity markets, but in the metals, currencies, interest rate futures, and stock market as well.

The idea that seasonal price patterns exist in virtually all cash and futures markets regardless of weather was a difficult one for many

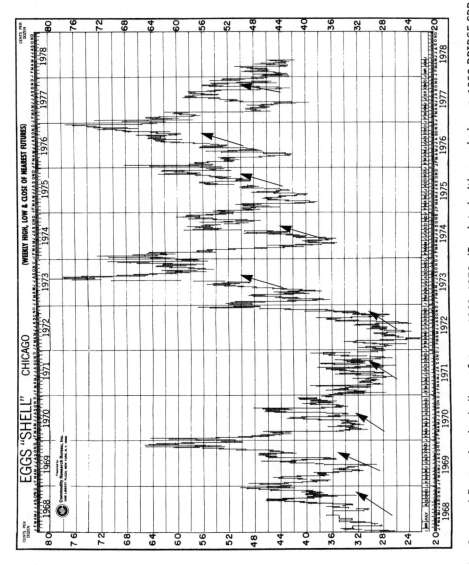

Figure 2-1 Seasonal fluctuation in shell egg futures, 1968–1978. (Reprinted with permission. © 1998 BRIDGE CRB, 30 South Wacker Drive, Suite 1810, Chicago, Illinois 60606.)

traders to accept. However, a growing body of solid statistical evidence, facilitated by computer technology, has supported the notion that there are numerous causes of seasonal price fluctuation in addition to weather. So, slowly but surely, the idea of seasonality as a price-shaping force *independent of weather* has taken root in the thinking of futures and stock traders.

Computer technology allowed a quantum leap in statistical research on seasonal behavior, as well as a concomitant increase in trading opportunities available to future traders. This book seeks to explain, evaluate, and introduce seasonal trading concepts from both an academic and pragmatic perspective. It explains the various aspects of seasonal price relationships—their use, limitations, and incorporation into various trading strategies.

PREVIOUS SEASONAL STUDIES AND RESEARCH

In Chapter 1, I referred to W. D. Gann, who was primarily interested in the pragmatic effects of seasonality on the price behavior of the grain and stock markets. In *How to Make Profits in Commodities* (Pomeroy, Wash.: Lambert-Gann, 1942), Gann described in detail his observation of the stock and commodity markets from a seasonal perspective. In some respects, Gann's work on seasonality stood for many years as the seasonal information that many traders talked about but with which they did little trading. The lack of action based on Gann's seasonal observations, however, did not denigrate the reality of seasonals.

In 1977, Larry Williams, an active stock and commodity trader since the 1960s with an international following, and Michelle Noseworthy published their findings on seasonal price fluctuations in the commodity futures markets. The results of their studies were impressive; in some cases, they showed, predictable price movements in certain futures markets had occurred more than 80 percent of the time over a 16-year period or more. Williams and Noseworthy were so convinced by their discoveries that they entitled their book on seasonals, *Sure Thing Commodity Trading.*[1]

The Williams and Noseworthy research represented a breakthrough

[1] L. Williams and M. Noseworthy, *Sure Thing Commodity Trading* (Brightwaters, N.Y.: Windsor, 1977).

in seasonal methodology. The authors brought to public attention a large number of price movements having a high probability of profitable results based on seasonal research. The seasonals were very specific, showing precise entry dates and exit dates, as well as an operational methodology for trade entry and exit. Of the "sure thing" seasonal tendencies given in their book, many have continued to follow the patterns that Williams and Noseworthy pointed out.

In 1977 also, I published a comprehensive study of seasonal price tendencies in the cash commodity markets. Using an extensive database of historical monthly cash market data, I constructed seasonal price tendency charts for a majority of cash markets and calculated monthly percentages of up-and-down price movements for the most actively traded market. Since the original publication of this report, I have updated it many times. Figures 2-2, 2-3, and 2-4 illustrate several monthly seasonal cash charts from the 1997 edition of this study.[2]

The current edition of my *Monthly Seasonal Cash Charts* employs a lengthy historical database, as well as a more refined analytical technique than used in my 1977 study. Many different approaches are possible in the analysis of seasonal price variation. I have developed a number of concise methods for depicting cash seasonal patterns in a variety of different ways so as to extract as much useful information from the data as possible. (Examples are given later in this book.)

Veteran trader and market analyst Perry Kaufman, in his classic book *Commodity Trading Systems and Methods* (New York: Wiley, 1978), highlighted a variety of seasonal approaches. That he included seasonality in his book did much to popularize the use of seasonals in futures trading, given his reputation in the futures industry.

Jack Grushcow and Courtney Smith, also known for their trading and research, likewise studied seasonal price behavior in the commodity market and published a fairly exhaustive analysis of seasonals in 1980 entitled *Profits Through Seasonal Trading* (New York: Wiley, 1980). Their technique analyzed fluctuation in cash and futures markets, culminating in a listing of up-and-down percentages for given months of the year in the commodity markets. Grushcow and Smith added considerable knowledge to the fund of seasonal data, supplying commodity traders with specifics on a monthly basis, as well as seasonal charts highlighting the major intrayear trends. To a certain extent,

[2]*MBH Monthly Seasonal Cash Charts* (Winnetka, Ill.: MBH Commodity Advisors, Inc., 1997).

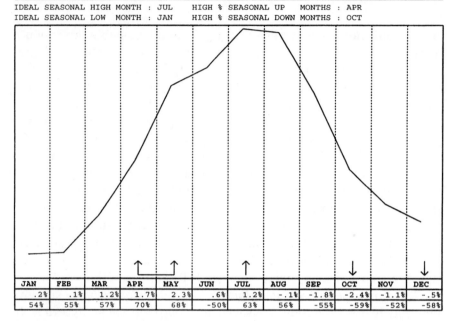

MONTHLY SEASONAL CASH TENDENCY: CORN   YEARS: 1720 - 1996
IDEAL SEASONAL HIGH MONTH : JUL   HIGH % SEASONAL UP   MONTHS : APR
IDEAL SEASONAL LOW MONTH : JAN   HIGH % SEASONAL DOWN MONTHS : OCT

JAN	FEB	MAR	APR	MAY	JUN	JUL	AUG	SEP	OCT	NOV	DEC
.2%	.1%	1.2%	1.7%	2.3%	.6%	1.2%	-.1%	-1.8%	-2.4%	-1.1%	-.5%
54%	55%	57%	70%	68%	-50%	63%	56%	-55%	-59%	-52%	-58%

Figure 2-2 Cash monthly seasonal tendency, corn, 1720–1996. (Copyright © 1997 by MBH Commodity Advisors, Inc.)

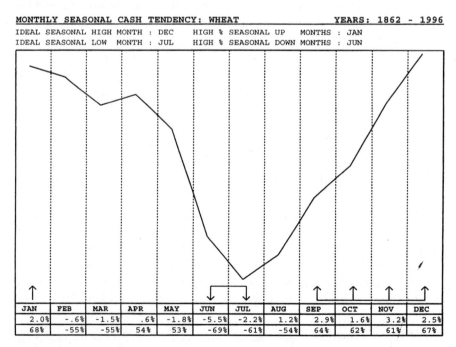

MONTHLY SEASONAL CASH TENDENCY: WHEAT   YEARS: 1862 - 1996
IDEAL SEASONAL HIGH MONTH : DEC   HIGH % SEASONAL UP   MONTHS : JAN
IDEAL SEASONAL LOW MONTH : JUL   HIGH % SEASONAL DOWN MONTHS : JUN

JAN	FEB	MAR	APR	MAY	JUN	JUL	AUG	SEP	OCT	NOV	DEC
2.0%	-.6%	-1.5%	.6%	-1.8%	-5.5%	-2.2%	1.2%	2.9%	1.6%	3.2%	2.5%
68%	-55%	-55%	54%	53%	-69%	-61%	-54%	64%	62%	61%	67%

Figure 2-3 Cash monthly seasonal tendency, wheat, 1862–1996. (Copyright © 1997 by MBH Commodity Advisors, Inc.)

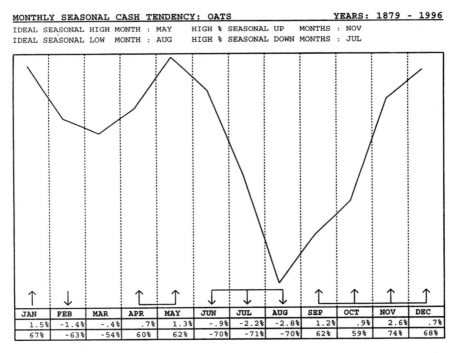

| MONTHLY SEASONAL CASH TENDENCY: OATS | | | | | | YEARS: 1879 - 1996 |

IDEAL SEASONAL HIGH MONTH : MAY   HIGH % SEASONAL UP   MONTHS : NOV
IDEAL SEASONAL LOW MONTH : AUG   HIGH % SEASONAL DOWN MONTHS : JUL

JAN	FEB	MAR	APR	MAY	JUN	JUL	AUG	SEP	OCT	NOV	DEC
1.5%	-1.4%	-.4%	.7%	1.3%	-.9%	-2.2%	-2.8%	1.2%	.9%	2.6%	.7%
67%	-63%	-54%	60%	62%	-70%	-71%	-70%	62%	59%	74%	68%

Figure 2-4 Cash monthly seasonal tendency, oats, 1879–1996. (Copyright © 1997 by MBH Commodity Advisors, Inc.)

these charts were similar in form to those I introduced in 1977 although their analytical methodology was somewhat different from mine.

WEEKLY SEASONAL PRICE PATTERNS

In 1983, I introduced the concept of weekly seasonal futures charts, my study of which provided commodity traders and commercials with a weekly chart for given futures contracts, illustrating the percentage of time prices had moved up or down and the average magnitude of the given move.[3] Traders around the world have used this study, updated every year since it first appeared, as a guide to shorter-term seasonals

[3]J. Bernstein, *Weekly Seasonal Futures Charts* (Winnetka, Ill.: MBH, 1983–1997).

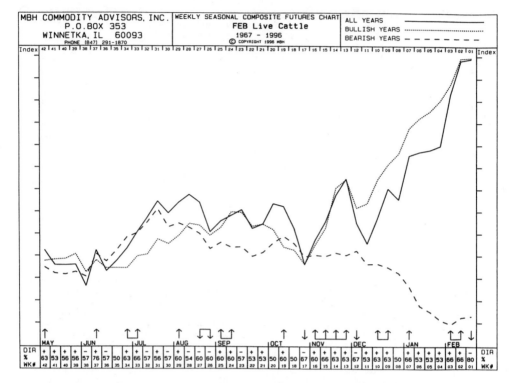

Figure 2-5   Weekly seasonal futures tendency, February live cattle, 1967–1996. (Copyright © 1996 by MBH Commodity Advisors, Inc.)

and as an adjunct to monthly seasonal cash charts. Figures 2-5 and 2-6 show some typical seasonal futures charts using my most up-to-date analytical methods, explained in detail later in the book.

The weekly listing allowed more precise timing of entry and exit by short-term traders. The weekly seasonal futures charts clearly demonstrated the specificity of given seasonal patterns within the year. Some price movements have been reliable over 80 percent of the time over a 27-year time span or longer. Highly predictable patterns on a weekly basis were isolated in virtually every futures market—metal, agricultural, and financial.

Of course, percentage readings in and of themselves can be illusory since they are dependent on the length of the database. A good statis-

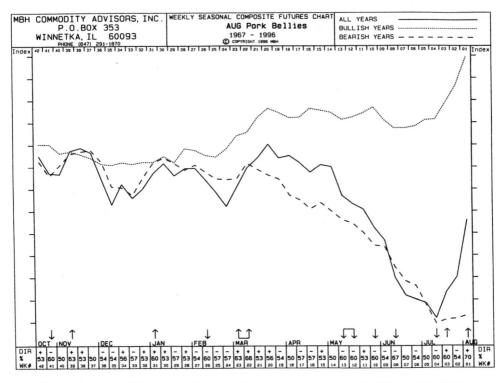

Figure 2-6 Weekly seasonal futures tendency, August pork bellies, 1967–1996. (Copyright © 1996 by MBH Commodity Advisors, Inc.)

tician would argue that various manipulations of data could yield a variety of results depending on what one wishes to show. It has been said, "Given enough statistics, you can prove anything." If, for example, I studied five years worth of data in lumber futures and showed that prices moved lower every time during the last two weeks of April, I could state that prices moved lower 100 percent of the time during the period studied over the time span of data; however, the length of my database would be too limited to allow for a valid conclusion.

If I used 10 years of historical data and showed that prices moved lower 10 out of 10 years during this time frame, then my 100 percent statistic would be more meaningful and reliable than the result based on 5 years of history. The longer a relationship lasts, the more statisti-

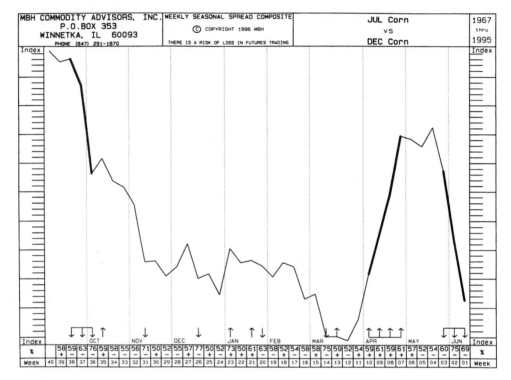

Figure 2-7 July versus December corn weekly seasonal composite spread, 1967–1995. (Copyright © 1996 by MBH Commodity Advisors, Inc.)

cally valid it is. The fewer data used in historical seasonal analysis, the less likely it is that a given percentage is valid and the more likely it is that the reading may be due to random fluctuation.

Some of the futures markets date back to the 1940s, and in some cases (wheat, corn, and oats) futures data are available back to the start of trading on the Chicago Board of Trade in the late 1800s. High weekly percentage up or down readings using such a lengthy data history add statistical validity to seasonal price patterns. Unfortunately, many futures markets have only limited data history.

As an outgrowth of my weekly seasonal charts, I applied the same analytical techniques to commodity spread data. In 1983, I published *How to Profit from Seasonal Commodity Spreads* (New York: Wiley), which illustrated that commodity spread (straddle) behavior also has

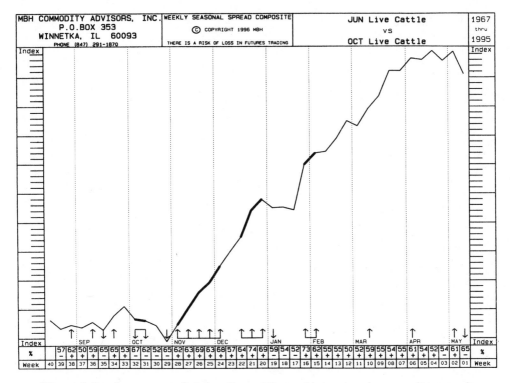

Figure 2-8 June versus October live cattle weekly seasonal composite spread, 1967–1995. (Copyright © 1996 by MBH Commodity Advisors, Inc.)

seasonal characteristics and, in some cases, these characteristics are more reliable (having occurred more often) than seasonal tendencies in net market positions. Commercial interests such as grain processors, livestock dealers, and meat packers have long used the seasonal price tendencies in their purchasing and hedging programs. *How to Profit from Seasonal Commodity Spreads* was updated and retitled as *Weekly Seasonal Spread Charts* (Winnetka, Ill.: MBH Commodity Advisors, Inc., 1983–1997). Figures 2-7, 2-8, and 2-9 contain seasonal spread charts showing a number of tendencies researched and highlighted in those charts.

In addition, I have developed several daily seasonal chart studies, as well as the key date seasonal methodology, all discussed in later chapters.

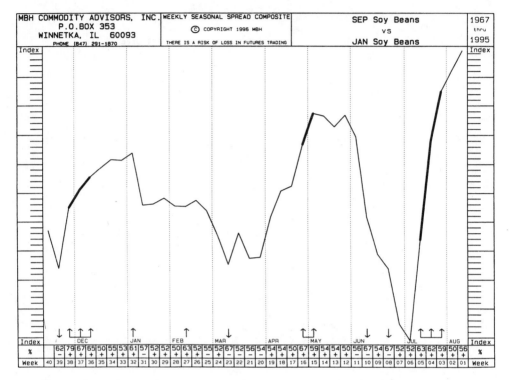

Figure 2-9 September versus January soybeans weekly seasonal composite spread, 1967–1995. (Copyright © 1996 by MBH Commodity Advisors, Inc.)

THE CURRENT STATUS OF SEASONAL PRICE RESEARCH

Although seasonality has become a more acceptable approach to futures analysis and market timing, relatively few solid research efforts are currently being carried out, for the following reasons:

1. Seasonality is still not widely accepted as a valid approach to stock and futures market analysis.
2. Seasonality is still not well understood by many traders. There is a tendency to confuse seasonality with weather-based price patterns, even though weather is only one aspect of seasonal price tendencies.

3. Some commodity options brokerage houses have heavily promoted seasonals, causing many uninformed investors to speculate in markets such as heating oil using seasonal research based on a narrow historical sample that was grossly insufficient with respect to validity. Hence, many investors have lost money using this information. As a result, the reputation of seasonality has been tarnished, causing investors and traders to shy away from seasonal methods. Moreover, the heavy promotion of limited history seasonals aroused the ire of government regulatory agencies, causing them to "throw out the baby with the bath water." Hence seasonals have a bad name.

4. A number of seasonal "researchers" have perpetuated the myth of seasonality by publishing seasonal trades based on limited data, exacerbating the negative reputation of seasonal analysis.

5. Although there have been many attempts to use seasonals effectively, there have been few valid studies on how to combine the high probability of seasonal with effective market timing methods. This limits the pragmatic application of seasonals.

6. There have been few courses or books that explain the use of seasonal methodologies and the logic of seasonal trading to traders.

Seasonal trading is a viable method when applied with consistency and specificity. As long as seasonal methods are combined with other techniques to confirm their validity, they have merit as valuable trading tools.

3

SEASONAL PRICE PATTERNS IN CASH MARKET DATA

Seasonal behavior can take many different forms. It is possible to study seasonal price fluctuation on a monthly, weekly, or daily basis. It is also possible to study seasonal price fluctuation in cash markets, futures markets, futures spreads, and a variety of economic data. In addition, one can evaluate the reliability of key date seasonal trades, anniversary date seasonal trades, and legal holiday seasonal patterns. There are as well various types of specialized indicators and variations on seasonal themes, such as the critical month indicator, a technique I developed as an outgrowth of my seasonal studies.

TYPES OF SEASONALS

Given the variety of seasonal methods, approaches, and directions, my first order of business is to familiarize you with different types of seasonals—their construction, use, limitations, and implications. Then this chapter focuses on cash seasonal tendencies in their various forms. I highlight the method by which cash seasonals are calculated and provide a list of the primary cash seasonal price tendencies in representative markets.

Monthly Seasonal Cash Analysis

This method of seasonal analysis uses monthly cash data, which often spans many years (in some cases several hundred years). Since the data are computed on a monthly basis, this approach allows only the determination of gross seasonal patterns. One benefit of using monthly cash prices for determining seasonals is that the ability to use a lengthy historical database increases the statistical reliability of the findings. A seasonal based on 200 years of data is more reliable than a seasonal based on only 25 years of data. The drawback of using monthly cash data is that they obscure seasonal patterns and moves that occur within a given month, as well as those that begin within one month and end within another.

Although the use of monthly cash data in determining seasonals is an excellent first step, it is a tool that is more suited for position traders, the hedgers, and producers since it provides only large-scale information. The results of seasonal cash studies can be used to discern global moves but not some of the shorter-term seasonal tendencies, which instead use weekly or daily seasonal tendencies.

Weekly Seasonal Futures Analysis

Weekly seasonal analysis uses weekly seasonal data in determining shorter-term seasonal tendencies. Although there are numerous ways in which the data can be handled, I prefer to calculate weekly seasonals on an end-of-week to end-of-week basis (say, Friday close to Friday close). Weekly seasonal analysis is best suited to position traders who wish to assess and trade with seasonal patterns that last from about one week to as long as five months.

The benefit of weekly seasonal analysis is that it provides shorter-term time frames for seasonal moves and can identify moves that will not appear in the monthly analysis. Thus, traders can better pinpoint their timing for market entry and exit. The disadvantage of using weekly seasonal futures data is that the data history in many cases is limited in length. In the energy futures markets, for example, the history goes back only to the 1980s when the futures markets for heating oil and crude oil were introduced. In the meat and livestock markets, the histories date back to the mid-1960s at best; the grain and soybean complex histories are considerably lengthier.

Daily Seasonal Futures Analysis

Daily seasonal analysis uses daily futures data to find short-term seasonal tendencies. Although there are numerous ways in which the daily data can be handled, I prefer to calculate daily seasonals on an end-of-day to end-of-day basis (say, Friday close to Friday close). Daily seasonal analysis is best suited to short traders who wish to assess and trade with seasonal patterns that last from about several days to several weeks.

The benefit of daily seasonal analysis is that it provides exact entry and exit dates for seasonal moves, and it identifies moves that will not appear in the weekly or monthly analysis. Thus, traders can better pinpoint their timing for market entry and exit. The disadvantage of using daily seasonal futures data is that the data history in many cases is limited in length, as it is in weekly futures seasonals. There are other limitations to the use of daily seasonal analysis, which are discussed in Chapter 6.

Weekly Seasonal Spread Analysis

Weekly seasonal spread analysis uses weekly seasonal data in determining seasonal spread tendencies. Although there are numerous ways in which the data can be handled, I prefer to calculate weekly spread seasonals on an end-of-week to end-of-week basis (say, Friday spread close to Friday spread close). Weekly seasonal spread analysis is best suited to position traders who wish to assess and trade with seasonal patterns that last from about one week to as long as five months.

The benefit of weekly seasonal spread analysis is that it provides shorter-term time frames for seasonal spread moves and identifies spread moves that do not appear in the monthly analysis. Traders can better pinpoint their timing for market entry and exit. The disadvantage of using weekly seasonal futures data for determining seasonal spreads is that the data history is limited in length in many cases.

Cash Seasonal High-Low Analysis

Another seasonal method with validity is to determine the most frequent months of the year during which highs and lows are made in the various commodity markets. This can be accomplished with cash or futures data; the cash market data have the longer history. This approach tells you which months of the year have shown the strongest tendencies for yearly highs and lows, information that is especially valuable to producers and hedgers who need to plan their purchases and sales. Speculators can also use these months along with market timing to enter or exit position trades.

Cash Seasonal Split-Decade Analysis

The split-decade seasonal method is used for examining the stability of cash seasonal patterns. It examines the monthly cash seasonal tendency on the basis of 10-year segments in order to see if seasonal patterns have changed appreciably over time.

Critical Seasonal Month Analysis

Critical seasonal month analysis is more of a technical timing method than a pure seasonal analysis method. Each market has one or several critical months—critical inasmuch as the penetration of its high and low prices has often triggered a strong move in the direction of the penetration. The specific rules to use in connection with this analysis are discussed in Chapter 7.

Key Date Seasonal Analysis

Of all the methods that may be used to analyze and trade seasonal patterns, this is the most controversial. This approach contends that there are specific dates of the year when markets move in given directions and that there are literally thousands of date combinations in all markets that have shown a high degree of reliability over a period of many years. The statistical reliability of this approach has been questioned. Furthermore, this method has aroused the ire of regulatory agencies in the futures industry inasmuch as various brokerage houses have used the statistics to advertise their services in a false or misleading way. Both of these issues, as well as the positive aspects of key date seasonal analysis, are discussed in Chapter 8.

SEASONALITY IN THE CASH MARKETS

For those who doubt the existence of seasonal tendencies in the futures markets, the study of cash seasonals over the past several hundred years will prove to be a most enlightening experience. While it could be argued that a seasonal pattern based on 5 or 10 or even 20 years is merely a random event—an artifact of the data—the longer the historical database under study is, the better the findings are in terms of statistical reliability. The issue of reliability is the single most pervasive and significant aspect of seasonal validity.

Those who question the existence and use of seasonals in a trading program or as a form of commodity market analysis point to the question of statistical validity as the central issue. I agree with them. However, there are several issues that must be taken into consideration before a trader can reach any conclusion about the validity of seasonals. There are also several levels on which such decisions can be made. Consider the following issues and decide how you align yourself.

Face Validity

Regardless of hard statistical evidence, one question that might be asked is whether the concept of seasonality has validity on the surface—on the face, that is. In other words, is it a reasonable and logical assumption—without solid statistical evidence—that seasonality exists in price patterns? Upon even minimal reflection the reply would be yes when you consider all the factors that might cause seasonal price patterns to exist—for example:

- Farmers in the United States harvest corn and soybean crops at about the same time of the year and bring them to market at about the same time of the year, thereby affecting prices.

- Cattle ranchers in the United States place cattle on feed at about the same time of the year and contract for their feed needs at about the same time of the year, thereby affecting prices of cattle as well as feed.

- Winter weather in the northern United States can reach as far south as the citrus-growing regions of Florida and Texas or as far west as California, resulting in frost or freeze and thereby affecting prices during certain times of the year.

- Builders buy lumber and other building supplies for the spring and summer building season late in the previous year, thereby affecting lumber and copper prices.

- Petroleum companies buy crude oil in the summer to have ample lead time to produce gasoline and heating oil for the winter. Prices usually rise from midsummer to late in the year.

- Investors tend to sell stocks toward year-end in order to take profits or losses for tax purposes. This affects prices toward year-end.

- Stock prices tend to rise a high percentage of the time on the day before major holidays in the United States. Various explanations have been offered for the existence of this phenomenon.

- The price of live hogs in the United States tends to rise from late October to early November as farmers harvest crops and cannot bring animals to market. This tends to reduce the available supply of animals and raises prices.

- Banks tend to invest funds and sell investments at certain times of the year based on consumer demand for money. This can affect interest rate trends.

- There has been a tendency for stock prices in the United States to reach low points on Monday. No firm explanation has been offered for this fact.

- There has been a tendency for coffee prices to rise from late in the year through March, during the height of the coffee-growing and -harvesting season in South America.

- There has been a strong tendency for the price of cattle futures to rally strongly once they penetrate their January high price or fall once they penetrate their January low price. No firm explanation can be offered.

- Wheat prices in the United States have often rallied from early July through November. This price rally often occurs while the price of corn is topping or moving lower.

- Gold prices have shown a tendency to rally from late August to late September. Various explanations have been advanced for this pattern.

Statistical Validity

The Foundation for the Study of Cycles in Wayne, Pennsylvania, has published many studies supporting the validity of seasonals. In addition to these, I have documented the existence of seasonality in many markets (as you will see later in this book). Ultimately, each trader must decide what constitutes sufficient validation for seasonality. If you are satisfied with a seasonal pattern that has been in existence for only 10 years, be aware that it may be a random event, and take adequate precautions in using that seasonal tendency. I address this issue more fully when I discuss the caveats of seasonal trading and research.

THE SEASONAL CONCEPT AS AN ADJUNCT OR AS A TECHNIQUE

Regardless of application or methodology, the concept of seasonality as an adjunct to trading may prove to be its most valuable application. Whether one subscribes to the specific methodologies described in this book or not, the existence of seasonality in terms of a general trend indicator can prove valuable as a filter or adjunct to other trading systems, technical as well as fundamental. In this respect, those who use the system must decide how best to integrate seasonals in their overall plan.

Some traders are more comfortable trading seasonal patterns that have face validity. In other words, they often feel more comfortable trading seasonals that have an observable pattern. The majority of seasonal patterns can be explained on the basis of fundamental underlying conditions. Although a purely technical trader may not require seasonals to have a basis in fact, the presence of an underlying cause helps add credibility as well as validity to the seasonals.

THE ADVANTAGES OF CASH SEASONAL PATTERNS

While it could be argued that there is a lack of sufficient historical data to analyze and evaluate many of the futures markets effectively, this is not a valid critique of cash seasonality. In analyzing cash market seasonals, I have used many years of historical data. In some markets, such as corn, the data history dates back to the early 1700s. In most cases, I have used as many historical data as are reasonably available and valid. Hence, the advantage of using cash data for the purpose of analyzing seasonal patterns is that the results will be more valid statistically than they would be with a shorter historical database.

The disadvantage of using monthly cash data for the purpose of analyzing seasonal trends is that the monthly data can reveal the gross aspects of seasonality on only a month-to-month basis. The finer details—in other words, the seasonal patterns—that occur during the month cannot be found using monthly data since the details are obscured by the monthly data.

Cash seasonals are an excellent starting point for the purpose of explaining and justifying the existence of seasonality and also for the purpose of finding larger patterns, which may then be refined using weekly and daily data. The progression used in this book is a logical way to develop and understand seasonality in the futures markets.

THE MONTHLY SEASONAL CASH CHART

Monthly cash seasonals are analyzed on the basis of monthly cash historical data. The analysis may be accomplished without a computer, although the use of a computer spreadsheet program, such as Microsoft Excel or Lotus 1-2-3, can greatly facilitate the process.

The most productive way to calculate cash seasonal tendencies is to use the average of price differences between specified units of time and calculate percentage up-and-down movement for each time segment over a given period of years. The technique proceeds according to the following steps:

1. Arrange the monthly cash data in an array format by month and year.

2. In arranging your data, list the years along the vertical axis and prices for the given months along the horizontal axis. This will allow for simple computation of price differences and average price differences.

3. Compute the differences across columns. The result will be a second array that lists only differences from one time span to the next. If, for example, you are working on the computation of monthly seasonal tendencies, you will be subtracting one month's reading from the next. For weekly figures, you would use weekly prices. Depending on your preference, you could use weekly average price, monthly average price, daily average price,

daily closing price, weekly closing price, or monthly closing price to make your computation. I prefer to look at average price as opposed to closing price; however, techniques differ according to different technical needs.

4. Calculate the sum of the price differences by algebraically adding all the price differences in the column, thereby arriving at an average of price differences. This figure shows the average magnitude of the price change for the price in question.

5. Determine the number of times that prices were up, down, or unchanged for the specified number of years or weeks. Steps 3 and 4 gave two important pieces of information: (1) the average price move and its algebraic sign and (2) the most frequent market direction. The result, when plotted in chart form, looks like Figure 3-1. The price line is a cumulative plot of the differences.

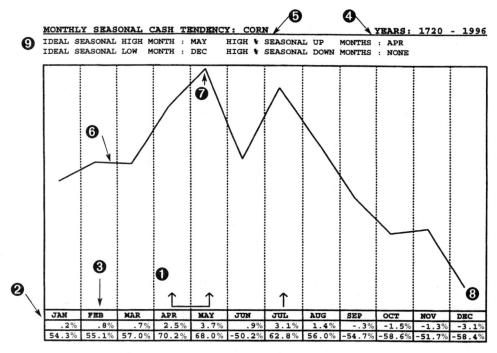

Figure 3-1 Sample monthly cash seasonal average price chart. (Copyright © 1997 by MBH Commodity Advisors, Inc.)

Explanation of Monthly Cash Seasonal Average Price Chart

The circled numbers in Figure 3-1 refer to the explanation that follows:

1. *Arrows.* The up and down arrows show the high historical percentage of time up or down (these are the best moves).

2. *Average percentage price change for the month during the years when the price changed.* The change is in the direction of the price plot. If the price plot is up from the previous price plot, then the percentage is up; if it is down, the percentage is down. Remember that this is an average figure based on many years of data. It is not necessarily indicative of the size move you can expect during any one month or year. Nevertheless, these figures can tell you when the big moves have happened on average historically.

3. *Month of the year.*

4. *Time span used for this chart.* Most markets show two time spans: the long-term seasonal tendency and the tendency from approximately 1960 to 1996 (unless otherwise indicated). Compare recent seasonals to longer-term seasonals for additional insight into market tendencies.

5. *Name of market.* (corn, live cattle, soybeans, etc.).

6. *Seasonal price plot line.* A cumulative price plot of the monthly average seasonal changes for the time span covered.

7. *Ideal seasonal high time frame.* The approximate time frame during which highs have been seen. There may be several seasonal highs or lows each year. Remember that these are *ideal* or *average* seasonal highs and lows and do not necessarily represent any one year for the given market.

8. *Ideal seasonal low time frame.* The approximate time frame of lows.

9. *Chart analysis.* A summary of the seasonal chart.

Figures 3-2 through 3-6 show a number of examples.

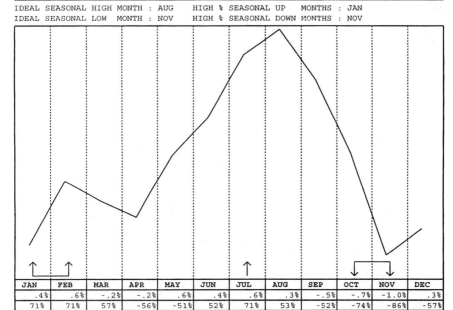

MONTHLY SEASONAL CASH TENDENCY: HOGS   **YEARS: 1891 - 1996**

IDEAL SEASONAL HIGH MONTH : AUG   HIGH % SEASONAL UP   MONTHS : JAN
IDEAL SEASONAL LOW MONTH : NOV   HIGH % SEASONAL DOWN MONTHS : NOV

JAN	FEB	MAR	APR	MAY	JUN	JUL	AUG	SEP	OCT	NOV	DEC
.4%	.6%	-.2%	-.2%	.6%	.4%	.6%	.3%	-.5%	-.7%	-1.0%	.3%
71%	71%	57%	-56%	-51%	52%	71%	53%	-52%	-74%	-86%	-57%

Figures 3-2   Monthly seasonal cash chart, hogs, 1891–1996. (Copyright © 1997 by MBH Commodity Advisors, Inc.)

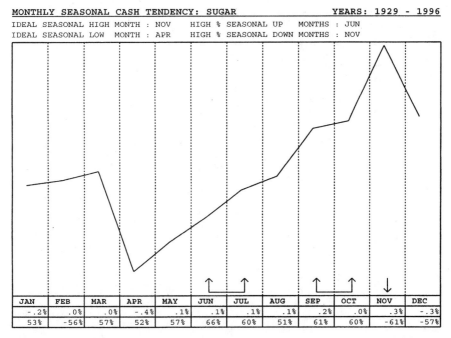

MONTHLY SEASONAL CASH TENDENCY: SUGAR   **YEARS: 1929 - 1996**

IDEAL SEASONAL HIGH MONTH : NOV   HIGH % SEASONAL UP   MONTHS : JUN
IDEAL SEASONAL LOW MONTH : APR   HIGH % SEASONAL DOWN MONTHS : NOV

JAN	FEB	MAR	APR	MAY	JUN	JUL	AUG	SEP	OCT	NOV	DEC
-.2%	.0%	.0%	-.4%	.1%	.1%	.1%	.1%	.2%	.0%	.3%	-.3%
53%	-56%	57%	52%	57%	66%	60%	51%	61%	60%	-61%	-57%

Figure 3-3   Monthly seasonal cash chart, sugar, 1929–1996. (Copyright © 1997 by MBH Commodity Advisors, Inc.)

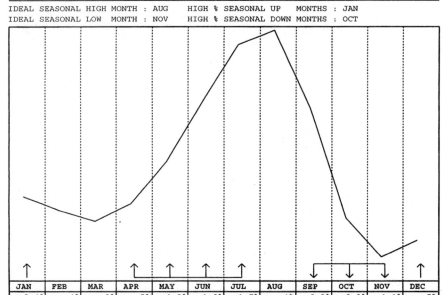

IDEAL SEASONAL HIGH MONTH : AUG   HIGH % SEASONAL UP   MONTHS : JAN
IDEAL SEASONAL LOW MONTH : NOV   HIGH % SEASONAL DOWN MONTHS : OCT

JAN	FEB	MAR	APR	MAY	JUN	JUL	AUG	SEP	OCT	NOV	DEC
2.4%	-.4%	-.3%	.5%	1.3%	1.8%	1.7%	.4%	-2.3%	-3.3%	-1.1%	.5%
78%	52%	-56%	60%	62%	71%	64%	-57%	-62%	-77%	-67%	58%

Figure 3-4   Monthly seasonal cash chart, pork bellies, 1949–1996. (Copyright ©
1997 by MBH Commodity Advisors, Inc.)

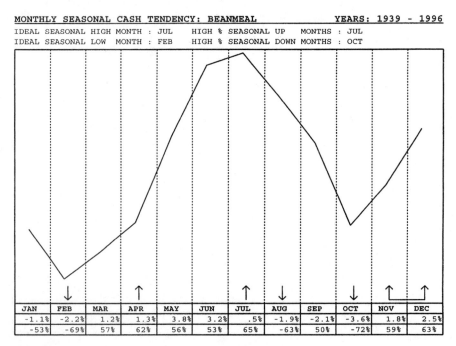

MONTHLY SEASONAL CASH TENDENCY: BEANMEAL   YEARS: 1939 - 1996
IDEAL SEASONAL HIGH MONTH : JUL   HIGH % SEASONAL UP   MONTHS : JUL
IDEAL SEASONAL LOW MONTH : FEB   HIGH % SEASONAL DOWN MONTHS : OCT

JAN	FEB	MAR	APR	MAY	JUN	JUL	AUG	SEP	OCT	NOV	DEC
-1.1%	-2.2%	1.2%	1.3%	3.8%	3.2%	.5%	-1.9%	-2.1%	-3.6%	1.8%	2.5%
-53%	-69%	57%	62%	56%	53%	65%	-63%	50%	-72%	59%	63%

Figure 3-5   Monthly seasonal cash chart, soybean meal, 1939–1996. (Copyright ©
1997 by MBH Commodity Advisors, Inc.)

MONTHLY SEASONAL CASH TENDENCY: COFFEE   YEARS: 1940 - 1996
IDEAL SEASONAL HIGH MONTH : JUN   HIGH % SEASONAL UP   MONTHS : JAN
IDEAL SEASONAL LOW MONTH : JAN   HIGH % SEASONAL DOWN MONTHS : JUL

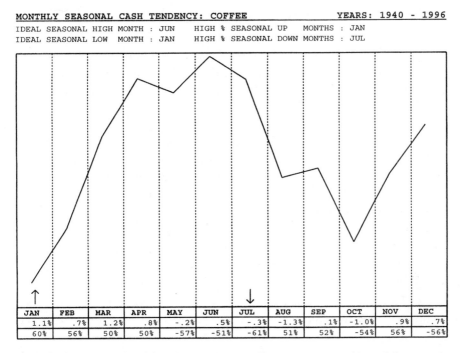

JAN	FEB	MAR	APR	MAY	JUN	JUL	AUG	SEP	OCT	NOV	DEC
1.1%	.7%	1.2%	.8%	-.2%	.5%	-.3%	-1.3%	.1%	-1.0%	.9%	.7%
60%	56%	50%	50%	-57%	-51%	-61%	51%	52%	-54%	56%	-56%

Figure 3-6 Monthly seasonal cash chart, coffee, 1940–1996. (Copyright © 1997 by MBH Commodity Advisors, Inc.)

A BRIEF DISCUSSION OF PROBABILITY

Statistics can be misleading. The old saying that "given enough statistics, you can prove anything" is probably an accurate commentary on the current fashion in which statistics are employed in the futures industry. When dealing with seasonal probability, it is important to distinguish the difference between *probability* and *history*. Although the history of a given market may have been highly repetitive, I caution against confusing history with probability. (Readers who are interested in the fine details of statistical analysis and probability are advised to consult books explaining statistics.) I prefer to classify the product of my seasonal research as a *tendency* rather than as a probability.

Clearly the more history one uses, the more confident one can be in the end result. Chapter 10 discusses the finer aspects of probability, tendency, seasonal odds, and statistical ramifications.

PRICE NORMALIZATION

Some analysts believe that it is important to evaluate seasonality by using normalized data rather than raw data to limit the effects of unusually large or small price movements during the data history. Price normalization can be achieved in either of two ways:

1. *Scale normalization.* Scale normalization is accomplished by inserting one step prior to the computation of the average seasonal price move. Whereas the percentage of time up or down remains the same, the price change itself is converted by using a percentage reading. To do this, scan the data price for a given time frame and find the lowest and highest entries. Now convert the lowest entry to 0 and the highest to 100. All other values will fall within the 0 to 100 range, which will minimize the distorting effect of unusually high or low values. After the data have been normalized, the computation of magnitude can be made.

2. *Percentage normalization.* Perhaps a more accurate and realistic normalizing technique is to compute percentage change within each time frame and then to average the percentage change figures. Let us say that the weekly closing price of market X this week is 60. The next week, prices close at 61. The net result is that prices have risen by l cent, or by 0.1667 percent. Instead of entering into the database the 1 cent price change, we enter the 0.1667 percent price change, since this yields a better representation as to the tendency of copper price magnitude during a given time span.

The preferable method is to calculate the percentage change in price during the time period being studied (weekly, daily, monthly) and then to take the percentage and magnitude averages of these computations to arrive at the measure of seasonal tendency. Although I have come to prefer the first approach, decide for yourself which technique better suits you.

Although the data in my examples are strictly price data, it is possible to analyze virtually any variable while studying for seasonality, regardless of whether it is price related.

4

SEASONAL PRICE PATTERNS IN WEEKLY FUTURES MARKET DATA

Chapter 3 discussed the computation of seasonal price tendencies in the cash markets. The technique is a simple one and can be adapted to the computation of daily, weekly, and spread seasonal futures tendencies. This chapter has three goals:

1. To isolate seasonal patterns in the futures markets and illustrate them in chart format.
2. To suggest several applications of futures seasonals in conjunction with trading systems or individually.
3. To illustrate weekly seasonal tendencies (where possible) specific to bull and bear trends.

The practical application of these charts and of seasonal tendencies is an individual matter. I reiterate that the material in this book is not a trading system. In the hope of facilitating the pragmatic and rational use of my results, I will give specific ideas as to how they may be employed.

The differences between these computations and those in the monthly cash charts are threefold:

1. Futures data are used in place of cash data.
2. Weekly or daily data are used instead of monthly data.
3. Friday to Friday (or last trading day of the week) prices are used in the weekly and daily futures seasonal analyses instead of average prices.

HOW TO DETERMINE THE SEASONALS

The seasonal readings tell us essentially the same thing on a weekly basis as did the cash figures on a monthly basis. The difference, of course, is that the weekly readings are shorter term and specific to a given futures contract. Anyone could construct a composite weekly seasonal picture for the entire year; however, as you will see later, this is not practical since markets are thinly traded prior to six months before contract expiration.

Here, step by step, is the basic procedure used in our computer analysis of seasonals:

1. Read the daily history file for each market and month for every year on file, (e.g., June live cattle, 1967, 1968, 1969, etc.).
2. Align each contract as closely as possible by date. The last day of trading is treated as day 1, the second day of last as day 2, etc. This is done since not all contracts terminate on the same precise calendar day. There are specific rules for determining last day of trading as set by the exchange, however, and most contracts terminate on or about the same week.
3. Calculate the price change for each week using the Friday price as the last price (or the last trading day of the week price if Friday was not a trading day). In so doing, we arrive at a weekly price change for each market and year.
4. Standardize or normalize the price changes for each year, to limit the effect of unusually large or unusually small price swings. We are primarily interested in direction of movement, or trend from one week to the next.
5. Calculate the algebraic average for each week. This yields an index of average weekly fluctuation.

6. Determine the percentage of years during which the price was up or down for given week.

7. Plot the cumulative price trend line and weekly percentage readings.

8. Determine bull, bear, or neutral status for each contract month for each market.

9. Repeat Steps 1 through 8 to plot weekly bull and bear market seasonals.

There are other ways in which the data could have been analyzed, and you may wish to experiment with different techniques of aligning the data or with different indexing methods.

Explanation of Weekly Seasonal Futures Chart

Figure 4-1 shows a typical seasonal futures chart with approximate week of year and percentage up or down tendency in the bottom row of the chart. The explanations that follow correspond to the numbers on the figure.

1. *Contract month and market that is plotted below.*

2. *Years covered for this chart.* Where a market has not been actively traded for too many years, there is less of a database, and therefore less reliability.

3. *Scale.* The normalized rate of change index that is used as a reference point. The scale values are not shown since they would be essentially meaningless inasmuch as they are of no specific value in using the seasonal trends other than to indicate average magnitude of change.

4. *Percentage of years up or down and arrows.* The weekly percentage of time up or down on a percentage basis, for the specific week number limited under the percentage reading. A reading of +75%, for example, indicates upward seasonality. Percentage readings from +60% to +100% indicate reliable bullish seasonals, and percentage readings from –60% to –100% indicate reliable bearish seasonals. Arrows up mark strong periods of bullish seasonality; arrows down mark periods of bearish seasonality.

Note also the following conditions:

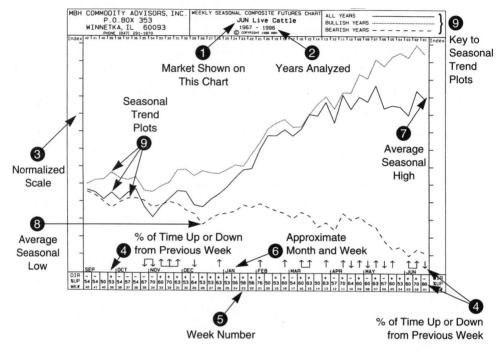

Figure 4-1 Sample weekly seasonal futures chart. (Copyright © 1996 by MBH Commodity Advisors, Inc.)

a. *When the plot is down and the percentage reading is +60% or higher,* this means that the market tends to move up during this approximate week more years than it moves down; however, the usual downmove is much larger than the net upmove, thereby accounting for the down plot. Upside potential during such weeks may be small in terms of magnitude, although downside moves can be large.

b. *When the plot is down and the percentage reading is –60% or more negative,* this means that the market has moved down 60 percent or more of the time for this approximate week during the years examined and that the size of the decline during down years is generally larger than the size of the rally during up years.

c. *When the plot is up and the percentage reading is –60% or more negative,* this is an indication that although most years are down for this approximate week, during those years that were up, the moves were relatively large. If you sell short on this type of combination, then you may take a very large risk for a potentially small, but reliable profit.

d. *The plot is unchanged (sideways) from previous week* indicates that the magnitude, or size, of the move for this approximate week is in equal balance between up and down. This does not necessarily mean a sideways trend for the week. Trend can be determined only by the accompanying percentage reading.

e. *If the percentage is +60% or more,* you can expect generally higher prices. If it is –60% or more negative, you can expect a downmove. The sideways plot means only that the up- and down-moves are about equal in size.

5. *Week number.* Under the percentage probability reading, the week number tells how many weeks are left to contract expiration. These are full weeks. A reading of 37, for example, means that this is approximately the thirty-seventh week before contract expiration. These figures are important in calculating the week number according to exchange expiration dates for any given year. Week numbers will allow you to determine relative time for any year. Remember that the month listings and number of weeks per month are approximate and that actual weeks will change somewhat each year. Note also that some contracts expire on the month before their listed month, (e.g., March sugar expires in February).

6. *Month and week.* The number of weeks in any given month, using Friday as the last day of a week, will vary from year to year. Sometimes November has five Fridays, and other years it has four. The weeks listed are only reference points. If you wish to adapt your chart for other trading years, determine when the contract is due to expire and work backward using the trading week as a guide. Once you have learned to use these charts, you will find that it is not necessary to pinpoint the exact week. If a market is conforming well to its seasonal trend, you can superimpose actual weekly price onto the seasonal chart and see whether there is a timing lead or lag. Use a clear acetate sheet for this purpose.

7. *Average seasonal high.* The average seasonal high is indicated by the highest plot on the chart. This means that during the years under study, there has been a tendency for prices to hit their contract

high around this week (or month). If a high is made during the last few weeks of a contract, then prices may move even higher several months thereafter, and the next contract month should be checked for this possibility. If a seasonal high is associated with high readings in the percentage column and a subsequent move to the downside occurs with equally reliable readings, then this is most likely a highly reliable seasonal top.

8. *Average seasonal low.* The indication of the average seasonal low means the same as average seasonal high, except in reverse.

9. *Plot.* The plot shows the seasonal tendency for all years (solid line), bull years (dotted line), and bear years (dashed line). The solid line is the most important one. The percentage up and down readings relate to the solid line (all years) plot.

RESEARCH ON SEASONALITY

The study and application of seasonality in the cash and futures markets is not new. Since the early 1970s various books, studies, and trading systems employing seasonal techniques as their basis have been published. In 1977 I published *Seasonal Chart Study, 1953–1977: Cash Commodities,* one of the first detailed studies that attempted to quantify seasonals in the commodity markets. Shortly after I published *Seasonal Chart Study II—Commodity Spreads,* which provided a week-by-week seasonal analysis of commodity spreads, isolating many highly reliable seasonal patterns. My spread book, *How to Profit from Seasonal Commodity Spreads* (New York: Wiley, 1990), gave specific instructions of many seasonal spreads.

Williams and Noseworthy, in their now-classic study of seasonal tendencies, *Sure Thing Commodity Trading,* provided traders with a list of specific seasonal trades that have demonstrated a high probability of recurrence.[1] Their concise study was a pioneering effort in isolating specific seasonal futures trades. In 1986, I wrote *Seasonal Concepts in Futures Trading* (New York: Wiley) to explain the tenets and applications of seasonality more fully. Recently I released High Odds Sea-

[1] L. Williams and M. Noseworthy, *Sure Thing Commodity Trading* (Brightwaters, N.Y.: Windsor, 1977).

sonal Trades computer software, which provides specific seasonal entry dates, exit dates, stop losses, and historical listings for about 27,000 of the most reliable seasonal trades.

The result of these and other research efforts, has been to increase trader awareness and use of seasonal price tendencies. Nevertheless, there are many detractors of seasonality. No matter how strong the statistical validation of seasonals may be, there are still those who doubt or impugn their value, and their attitudes have infiltrated the highest levels of the futures industry—even the regulatory agencies.

There are few traders who can use seasonal concepts to their advantage. There are numerous reasons for the limited use of seasonal tendencies. In addition to ignorance and lack of discipline, futures traders often abuse seasonal patterns, employing them in a fashion that may not be consistent with the optimum or intended applications of seasonality.

Consequently, traders often seek to justify an already established position by referring to seasonals. If the seasonal does not agree with their opinion, they ignore the seasonal; if there is agreement, they may add to their position. There are also traders who understand the concept of seasonality and are aware of its value but do not have the patience to trade effectively. These are primarily problems of discipline and will not be discussed in this book.

THE SEASONAL RUN

Seasonal run (SR) refers to a period of weeks during which a high-reliability seasonal move tends to occur. The SR is arbitrarily defined as a period of weeks that in succession (or close succession) read 59 percent reliability or more. An SR may not have more than two intervening weeks between high-reliability readings of less than 59 percent. Some markets exhibit a significant tendency toward SRs; others show only individual weekly seasonal tendencies having high reliability.

Figures 4-2, 4-3, and 4-4 show seasonal price charts with high-reliability SRs. Arrows delineate these time frames, with the direction of the arrow showing the SRs to the upside or downside. (Appendix C provides weekly seasonal price charts for futures contracts that are reasonably representative of the various futures markets.)

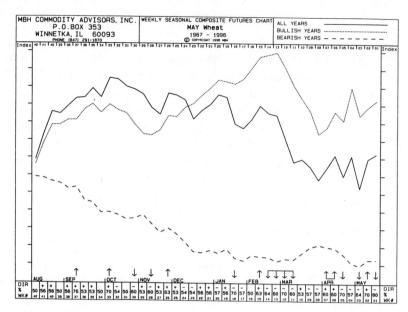

Figure 4-2 Seasonal tendency and seasonal run in May wheat, 1967–1996. Note the February–March (Weeks 14 through 11) run. (Copyright © 1996 by MBH Commodity Advisors, Inc.)

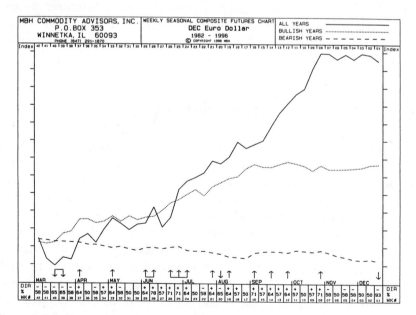

Figure 4-3 Seasonal tendency and seasonal run in December Eurodollar, 1982–1996. Note Weeks 29 through 21. (Copyright © 1996 by MBH Commodity Advisors, Inc.)

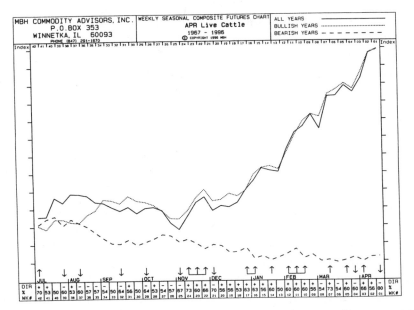

Figure 4-4   Seasonal tendency and seasonal run in April live cattle, 1967–1996. Note Weeks 17 through 7. (Copyright © 1996 by MBH Commodity Advisors, Inc.)

All of the seasonal charts, computations, seasonal runs, and reliability readings in this book are computed only through 1996. In order to have up-to-date information on the seasonals, you will need to use current data and recalculate the seasonal tendencies after each additional year's worth of futures data. This is a procedure that all serious traders should regularly observe in computing seasonals since each additional amount of data may alter the given seasonal tendency. At times it will confirm a seasonal run, and at times it may negate its validity.

A MORE OPERATIONAL DEFINITION OF SEASONALITY

Commodity markets move in fairly regular price patterns. To most traders, these periodic or cyclical movements are not meaningful since they are not obvious. This is truly unfortunate since regularity and repetition are the cornerstones of profitable trading. All trading systems seek to isolate patterns, signals, or indicators that repeat frequently enough and with sufficient reliability to permit profitable trading. Seasonals and cycles are the quintessential factors underlying market regularity.

Those who have read my *Commodities Now Through 1984* (Winnetka, Ill.: MBH Commodity Advisors, Inc., 1987), *Futures—Now Through 2001* (Winnetka, Ill.: MBH Commodity Advisors, Inc., 1987), and *Cycles Through 2010* (Winnetka, Ill.: MBH Commodity Advisors, Inc., 1991) should be familiar with the basic long-term cycles in each market. Although some of the forecasts have not yet come to pass, many—even some of my more radical expectations—have become realities during the past few years. This attests to the validity of cycles. Within the long-term cyclical patterns, we find shorter-term repetitions in price trend. Among these are included seasonal price patterns and short-term cycles.

Comparing all existent market patterns would permit virtually errorless forecasting of process. Our ability to recognize and use all of the relevant price inputs, however, is limited; hence, our forecasting ability is diminished. Inasmuch as seasonal factors affect prices, it is possible (or should be) to determine if and when a given market will move up or down due to seasonality. A seasonal pattern is therefore the tendency of a given futures market to trend in a given direction at certain times of the year.

USING THE WEEKLY FUTURES SEASONAL CHARTS

You do not need a background in computer programming to understand the manner in which the statistical data for this book were prepared. In order for you to understand the results and the intensity of effort that was involved in analyzing the seasonals, I suggest you familiarize yourself with the methodology used.

Remember that these charts are composites—a combination of many years of prices. We can then reasonably assume that the current trends will be the most reliable factor in a market, as opposed to seasonality. We can also assume that once a trend starts, it should continue. It is best not to rely on seasonals when this occurs. Note also that relative highs and lows within the composite chart are not necessarily repeated in any actual year's market. Some years may look exactly like

the seasonal composite charts, and others may not. A low may or may not occur at a given time period. This does not mean, however, that the seasonal chart is not valid.

In using these charts, there are several things you should be aware of:

- *Very strong up or down weeks* are weeks with readings in excess of 70%.

- *During long-term up- or downtrends,* seasonals consistent with the existing trend should perform well.

- *Average seasonal highs and lows* can be estimated by reference to the chart and in accordance with the guidelines outlined previously.

- *Contraseasonal moves* in the actual market can be spotted. If a particular market shows highly reliable seasonality on the composite and this pattern fails to appear in the actual market for a particular year, then a further move in the contraseasonal direction can be expected. This is perhaps one of the most important uses of a seasonal chart.

- *Market turns* can be expected at certain times of the year. If the market is moving down and the seasonal chart shows a very high percentage reliability downmove followed by a large upmove reliability, look for a trend change in the market.

There are many other uses for these data; applications are limited perhaps only by your imagination and resourcefulness. I believe that they are best used in conjunction with trading systems—technical or fundamental. Some market students have asked me whether I consider this type of information to be technical or fundamental in nature. My response is that this is perhaps the most important fundamental information that can be obtained in technical market studies.

HOW TO USE SEASONAL COMPOSITES WITH YOUR TRADING SYSTEM

Here are a few general suggestions as to how this information might be useful in your trading program:

- *Point and figure charting, bar charting, close-only charts, and moving averages.* Seasonals can help some trading systems do their best work. When seasonals are in reliable trends, other indicators are often more effective. If you get a signal to buy during a period that is clearly bearish on the seasonal composite chart, be careful. You might want to test the history of your trading system against the seasonal indications. If you find that many or most of your losses and incorrect signals come during seasonal moves in the opposite direction, then you might do well to build a seasonal filter into your system.

- *Moving averages.* These can help isolate the start of a seasonal. If there has been a fairly consistent uptrend, for example, and we are entering a period of seasonal highs, we can be quite certain that the moving average signals will be reliable as soon as the seasonal composite shows the start of a reliable downtrend. When seasonals and moving averages work together, the outcome tends to be more reliable.

- *Hedging and spreading.* Hedgers may wish to use the seasonal highs and lows as points for market entry and exit. Spread traders can determine the relative relationship between two contracts in a given market at similar times of the year and/or the relationship between different markets during the same period (e.g., corn versus wheat from October through December). Spread traders can also use seasonal spread charts.

- *Fundamentalists should be aware of the seasonals.* Bearish news at seasonal lows often fails to result in lower prices, and vice versa at seasonal highs with bullish news. Inasmuch as seasonality is a fundamental factor, those who trade from such an orientation should also consider the role of seasonals. Do not buck the seasonal trend, regardless of fundamentals, particularly if the seasonal pattern is highly reliable.

MORE DETAILS ABOUT THE SEASONAL FUTURES CHARTS

The seasonal chart methods do not provide specific trading signals; what they can help you do is make high-probability seasonal moves. The chart points were calculated on a Friday-to-Friday basis (last trading day of the week through last trading day next week). If a given

week shows strong upside reliability, consider buying on the Friday's close, before the coming week, and selling out on the next Friday's close. If you do this, your results will most likely reflect the seasonal chart patterns. Some traders use the seasonal patterns for market entry and exit at key turning points. Their overall results may be better than those of individuals who trade only the weekly moves, based on percentages, yet there are no prescribed or preferred techniques. You must develop your own applications.

Here are a few further details regarding the weekly seasonal futures charts:

- Reliability figures show the percentage of weeks that price closed up or down from the previous week.
- Be especially careful not to take very high or low readings too seriously if they were computed on a limited number of history years. The more years used in the analysis, the more meaningful and reliable the readings are.
- The weekly percentage reading and how it relates to current time.

The weekly readings have been obtained by aligning the contract data from last trading day to first trading day. The month and week readings listed along the bottom of each chart are only reference points; they do not necessarily apply to every calendar year. In future years or past years, there may be several weeks' shift in timing. In such cases, you can determine the correct week and month by working backward from the last entry (lower right-hand portion of the chart) and counting the week numbers to current time. Simply determine from the exchange rules (or from your broker's information) when a given contract is due to expire, and make your determinations accordingly. After some practice, you will be able to isolate the period rather easily. Your analyses will help you know if there has been a lead or lag in the current contract.

DISTORTION OF SEASONALS AT MAJOR CYCLICAL TOPS AND BOTTOMS

Seasonal price patterns are by no means the only reliable market cycles. At major long-term tops and bottoms, seasonal cycles may be distorted. If you are aware of the long cyclical term patterns within which seasonals function, you can be well prepared for a time when seasonals may become unreliable.

Remember, above all, that when one extracts a part from the whole, an unnatural distortion of the original data may result. Extracting seasonals and using them regardless of cycles and trends can distort them. Consequently, when the analysis is over and you have gleaned the necessary information, the part must be replaced within the whole. A total picture is necessary in the formulation of any long-range decision. Students of seasonals should also be students of cycles.

LIMITING YOUR LOSSES

One of the most serious errors a trader can make is to become totally dependent on a single method or technique. We do not yet have seasonal trading tools that are totally reliable. When you make trades, *use stop losses and limit your risk.*

THE BULL AND BEAR MARKET PLOT CHARTS

The charts have three price plots: bullish years, bearish years, and all years. Following are the factors I used in my bull and bear market selection:

1. *Daily closing direction.* Closing prices were examined daily and tallied as to higher close or lower close. A higher percentage of up closes compared to down closes was considered bullish. A higher percentage of down closes compared to up was considered bearish.

2. *Daily price change summation.* Daily price change and direction of change were summed. If the sum of plus changes was greater than the sum of minus changes, bull market status was assigned. The opposite situation meant a bear market.

3. *Closing price versus nine-day moving average (MA).* The total number of days' close above the nine-day MA was compared to the total number of days' close below the nine-day MA. If total closes above the nine-day MA was greater than the total closes

below the nine-day MA, the market was defined as bullish. If the total number of closes below the nine-day MA was greater, the market was defined as bearish.

4. *Closing price versus four-day MA.* The same rules apply as in rule 3 but using four-day MA.

5. *Closing price versus open price summation.* This variable compares daily closing price to daily opening price. Each instance of close greater than open was considered a bull market factor; each instance of close less than open was considered a bear factor. If total closes greater than opens was larger than total closes less than open, the market trend was considered bullish, and vice versa.

6. *Closes above or below channel index.* This factor compares the total number of closes above my proprietary channel index to the total number of closes below the channel index. If closes above were greater than closes below, this was considered bullish, and vice versa.

If four of the above six factors were positive, the market trend was defined as bullish; if four of six were negative, the trend was defined as bearish. If the split was three and three, the market was termed neutral and dropped from the analysis. If a bull or bear plot is not shown on a chart, there were insufficient data to permit such a plot. Note that the percentage readings in the charts apply only to the "all years" plot. There are no percentage listings for the bull or bear plots. Note also that neutral (no trend) years were dropped from the bull and bear plots but *are* included in the "all years" plot.

WHAT YOU SHOULD KNOW ABOUT STATISTICAL RELIABILITY AND THE SEASONAL CHARTS

The study of statistics is primarily concerned with such issues as determining whether given events are random (chance) occurrences or if they are predictable events that are a function of some underlying causal or correlation factor(s). A good statistician will tell you that the more observations you make of a given event, the more information you will have regarding the repetitive or random nature of that event.

In the case of a coin toss, for example, the outcome of each toss is independent of the outcome of previous tosses, assuming an unbiased coin. Therefore, even if you have tossed 10 successive heads, there is no guarantee that the next toss will be a head or a tail. Assuming that the coin is not improperly weighted or intentionally designed to show a preference, the results of each loss are purely random.

Certain events are not random; they do, in fact, show repetitive patterns. However, it is impossible to know exactly how repetitive they are until we closely examine them mathematically. In order to do so, we need considerable data—a challenge for the futures analyst inasmuch as there are only limited data available in many of the markets. In the meat and livestock markets, for example, futures trading began in the 1960s. In the grain and soybean complex, there are considerable data, as far back as the late 1800s. But in some of those years, trading volume was very thin, contract months differ somewhat from current standards, and daily price ranges were very small in many cases.

Clearly the issue is whether to test as many valid data as we have, devise a different type of statistical test, or not use the data at all. The third choice—not using the data for assistance in making trading decisions—is out of the question. To use and test the data we have available is the only alternative. Although not everyone will be pleased with the statistical limitations of my study, it is the only viable alternative of the few available choices, and so you must use my results, with these limitations clearly in mind.

EXAMPLE OF SEASONAL APPLICATIONS

There are various applications of seasonal price tendencies. Here is one example of how the information might be used.

Assume that you wanted to filter a seasonal trade using a timing indicator. In other words, you will want to go short April cattle futures as soon as a timing indicator has turned bearish. You will do this since you know that seasonal timing is not right 100 percent of the time, and adding a timing filter to the seasonal tendency could improve your timing.

Consult your favorite timing signal(s). For the sake of illustration, I will select an 18-day MA as the timing tool. Typically closes below the 18-day MA are bearish, and closes above it are bullish. An exami-

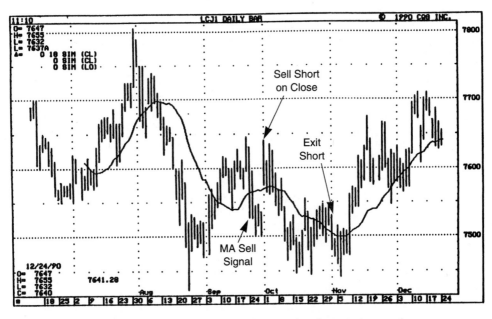

Figure 4-5   Daily April 1991 live cattle futures showing 18-day moving average and seasonal entry and exit. (Reprinted with permission of CQG, Inc.)

nation of the relevant price chart (see Figure 4-5) shows an example of this approach.

Remember that this scenario was reconstructed with the aid of hindsight, and your decisions in an actual application might have been different. This is why I suggest that you develop your own style and applications for the seasonal data.

5

SEASONAL SPREAD RELATIONSHIPS

In *How to Profit from Seasonal Commodity Spreads* (New York: Wiley, 1983), I outlined in considerable detail the technique by which seasonality is determined for commodity spreads and the method by which it is employed in a trading method. Average or novice traders do not ordinarily attempt commodity spread trading; however, it is a reliable and potentially profitable technique when used with seasonal tendencies and patterns.

Weekly seasonal spread patterns tend to repeat with a relatively high degree of accuracy. In order to discern spread seasonals, I use a weekly seasonal composite spread chart, constructed in a fashion similar to what has already been discussed for weekly seasonal futures charts, with the percentage readings used in approximately the same fashion. In spread trading, of course, you are dealing with two futures contracts rather than one. The price plot on the spread composite chart indicates a particular contract's gaining or losing in price relationship to another contract. Hence, the difference between two prices is what a spread plots.

TERMINOLOGY

A *spread* involves two sides or legs—one long and one short. The first contract month listed is the *buy,* or *long,* leg of the spread, and the second month listed is the *sell,* or *short,* leg. Thus, the July/December corn spread is defined as long July versus short December.

Intracommodity spreads are those in two different contract months of the same market, such as July/December wheat. The majority of spread seasonal charts in this book are *intercommodity spreads*—those in two different but usually related markets, such as July corn/July oats. Such spreads may involve more risk than intracommodity spreads. I have included most of the well-known intercommodity spreads, as well as a few that have not had too much of a following but appear to have a strong seasonal uptrend, interrupted by only a few low-reliability readings. Longer-term traders might establish and hold a position through this seasonal uptrend. Watch for these runs. They often pinpoint the most reliable seasonal moves.

Seasonal spread patterns are by no means the only reliable market patterns. At major long-term tops and bottoms, seasonal spreads may be distorted. If you are aware of the long cyclical term patterns within which seasonals function, you can be prepared well in advance for a period of time during which spread seasonals may become unreliable. A total picture is necessary in the formulation of any long-range decision. Students of seasonals should also strive to be students of cycle and timing indicators, which may confirm the validity of the seasonal and assist with timing.

HISTORY OF WEEKLY SEASONAL SPREAD CHARTS

The seasonal futures spread charts I have shown in this book were produced with up-to-date futures prices. In cases where history was extremely limited, thereby making seasonal spread computations unfeasible, charts were not produced, since the seasonal readings and conclusions derived from them would be essentially meaningless.

My charts may differ from seasonal spread charts derived using different analytical methods from mine. Remember that seasonal percentage readings do not constitute sure things, no matter how high readings may be. Seasonality is merely an indicator of what has happened in the past. The seasonal percentage readings and charts contained in this book do not constitute a trading system; rather, they are intended to serve as analytical tools.

DETERMINING THE SPREAD SEASONALS

It is not necessary to have a background in computer programming to understand the manner in which the spread data for this study were prepared. Here, step by step, is the basic procedure used in my computer analysis of seasonal spreads:

1. Calculate the daily spread differential for all spreads being studied (e.g., June versus December live cattle, 1967, 1968, and so on).

2. Align each contract as closely as possible by date. The last day of trading is treated as day 1, the second day of trading as day 2, and so on. This is done since not all contracts terminate on the same calendar day. There are specific rules for determining the last day of trading as set by the exchange, however, and most contracts terminate on or about the same week.

3. Calculate the spread change for each week using the Friday price as the last price (or the last trading day of the week price if Friday was not a trading day). In so doing, you arrive at a weekly spread change for each market and year.

4. Standardize or normalize the weekly spread changes for each year. This is done to limit the effect of unusually large or unusually small swings. You are primarily interested in the direction of move or trend from one week to the next.

5. Once data have been normalized, calculate the algebraic average for each week. This yields an index of average weekly fluctuation.

6. Determine the percentage of years during which the spread was up or down for the given week compared to the previous week.

7. Plot the cumulative spread trend line (seasonal spread trend) and weekly percentage readings.

There are other ways in which the data could have been analyzed. If you plan to replicate this study with your own database, you may wish to experiment with different techniques of aligning the data or with different indexing methods.

HOW TO READ THE SEASONAL FUTURES SPREAD CHARTS

Figure 5-1 shows a sample seasonal spread chart. The numbers on it correspond to the following key points:

1. *The contract month and spread plotted below.*

2. *Years covered for this seasonal spread chart.* For this chart, the years 1970 through 1995 were used. Where a market has not been actively traded for too many years, there is less of a database, and therefore less reliability.

3. *Scale.* This is the normalized rate of change index that is used as a reference point. The scale values are not shown since they would be essentially meaningless; they are of no specific value in using the seasonal trends other than to indicate average magnitude of change.

4. *Percentage of years up or down and arrows.* These figures show the weekly time up or down on a percentage basis for the week number listed under the percentage reading. If the data plot (see point 9) for a given week is up from the previous plot and the reading is +75%, for example, this is an indication of upward seasonality for the indicated spread.

Percentage readings from +59% to +100% indicate reliable bullish seasonals; percentage readings from −59% to −100% indicate reliable bearish seasonals. Arrows up mark strong periods of bullish seasonality; arrows down mark periods of bearish seasonality.

Note also the following conditions:

a. *The plot is down and the percentage reading is +59% or more higher.* This means that the spread tends to move up during this approximate week more years than it moves down; however, the usual downmove is much larger than the net upmove, thereby accounting for the down plot. Upside potential during such weeks may be small in terms of magnitude, although upside moves can be large.

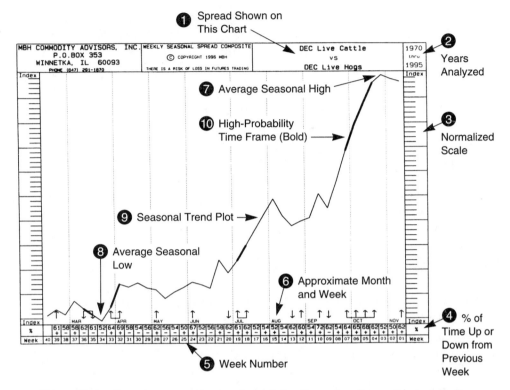

Figure 5-1 Sample seasonal spread chart for December live cattle versus December live hogs chart. (Copyright © 1996 by MBH Commodity Advisors, Inc.)

b. *The plot is down and the percentage reading is –59% or more negative.* This means that the average seasonal spread high is indicated by the highest plot on the chart. During the years under study, there has been a tendency for prices to hit their contract high around this week and/or month.

If a high is made during the last few weeks of a contract, then prices may move even higher several months after, and the next contract month should be checked for this possibility. If a seasonal high is associated with high readings in the percentage column and a subsequent move to the downside occurs with equally reliable readings, this is most likely a highly reliable seasonal top.

c. *The plot is up and the percentage reading is 59% or more negative.* This is an indication that although most years are down, for those years that were up, the moves were relatively large. If you sell short on this type of combination risk, you will have a potentially small but reliable profit.

d. *The plot is unchanged (sideways) from the previous week.* This is an indication that the magnitude, or size of the move, for this appropriate week is in equal balance between up and down. This does not necessarily mean a sideways trend for the week. Trend can be determined only by the accompanying percentage reading. If it is 59% or more, you can expect generally higher prices. If it is –59% or more negative you can expect a down-move. The sideways plot means only that the up- and down-moves are about equal in size.

5. *Week number.* This number tells how many weeks are left to contract expiration. These are full weeks. The last full week of trading would read 1 since it is the final full week in the life of the contract. A reading of 25, for example, means that this is approximately the twenty-fifth week prior to contract expiration.

These figures are important in calculating the week number according to exchange expiration dates for any given year. Note that these week numbers will allow you to determine relative time for any year. Remember that the month listings and number of weeks per month are approximate and that the actual weeks will change somewhat each year.

6. *Month and week.* The number of weeks in any given month, using Friday as the last day of a week, will vary from year to year. Sometimes November will have five Fridays, and other years it will have four. The weeks listed are only reference points. If you wish to adapt your chart for other trading years, determine when the contract is due to expire and work backward, using the trading week as a guide.

Once you have learned to use these charts, you will find that it is not necessary to pinpoint the exact week. If a market is conforming well to its seasonal trend you can superimpose actual weekly price onto the seasonal chart and see whether there is a timing lead or lag. Use a clear acetate sheet for this purpose.

7. *Average seasonal spread high.* This is indicated by the highest plot on the chart. This means that during the years under study, there has been a tendency for prices to hit their contract high around this

week or month. If a high is made during the last few weeks of a contract, then prices may move even higher several months thereafter, and the next contract month should be checked for this possibility. If a seasonal high is associated with high readings in the percentage column and a subsequent move to the downside occurs with equally reliable readings, this is most likely a highly reliable seasonal top.

8. *Average seasonal spread low.* The same holds true for seasonal low, only in reverse.

9. *Plot.* This line shows the weekly composite seasonal tendency for the indicated spread.

10. *Bold lines.* These denote high-probability time frames.

Figure 5-2 shows a sample chart for soybeans versus wheat.
In using these charts there are several things you should look for:

- *Very strong up or down weeks.* When I say *strong,* I mean reliabilities in excess of 59 percent over 10 years or more.
- *Long-term trends.* During long-term up or down trends, seasonals consistent with the existing trend should perform well.
- *Seasonal highs and lows.* Seasonal highs and lows can be estimated by reference to the chart and in accordance with the guidelines outlined previously.
- *Contraseasonal moves.* Contraseasonal moves in the actual spread can be spotted. If a particular spread shows highly reliable seasonality on the composite spread chart and if this pattern fails to appear in the actual spread for a particular year, then a further move in the contraseasonal direction can be expected. This is perhaps one of the most important uses of a seasonal chart.
- *Market turns.* Market turns can be expected at certain times of the year. If the spread is moving down and the seasonal spread chart shows a very high percentage reliability downmove followed by a large upmove reliability, look for a trend change in the market.

There are many other uses. Applications of these data are limited only by your imagination and resourcefulness. I believe that these charts are best used in conjunction with trading systems, either technical or fundamental.

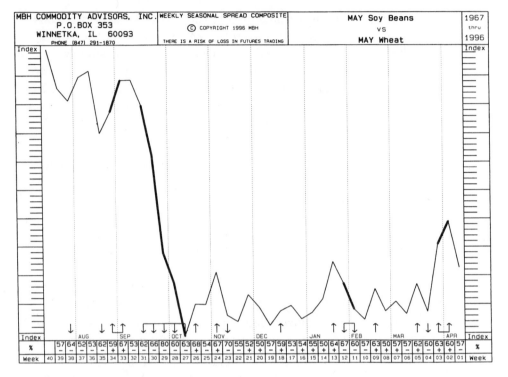

Figure 5-2   Seasonal spread chart for May soybeans versus May wheat, 1967–1996. (Copyright © 1996 by MBH Commodity Advisors, Inc.)

MORE DETAILS ABOUT THE SEASONAL FUTURES SPREAD CHARTS

It is *not* the intention of this chart study to provide spread trading recommendations; rather, it is to help you make effective decisions. The chart points were calculated on a Friday-to-Friday basis (last trading day of the week through last trading day next week). If a given week shows strong upside reliability, then you might consider entering the indicated spread on the Friday previous to the coming week and exiting the spread on the next Friday.

In so doing, your results will most likely reflect the idealized chart results. Some people use the seasonal spread charts for market entry at key turning points. Their overall results may be better than those of individuals who trade only the weekly moves, yet there are no prescribed or preferred techniques. You must develop your own applications.

Remember that these charts are composites, or a combination of many years of prices. As such, extreme highs and extreme lows during the same period of time in different years tend to balance each other out, and the net result will be a relatively even line on the seasonal chart. This is valuable information since it shows that the market is not seasonal at given times of the year. We can then reasonably assume that the existing trend will be the most reliable factor as opposed to seasonality. We can also assume that once a trend starts, it should continue.

It is best not to rely on seasonals when this occurs. Note also that relative highs and lows within the composite chart are not necessarily repeated in any actual year's market. Some years may look exactly like the seasonal composite charts, and others may not. A low may or may not occur at a given time period, but this does not mean that the seasonal spread chart is not valid.

Here are a few further details regarding this study. Please read carefully since they contain information you may need in your use of the charts.

Organization of charts. The charts are organized by market groups in chronological order by contract month.

Reliability reading. These figures show the percentage of weeks that the indicated spread closed up or down from the previous week. There are some weekly reliability readings of 100% or 0% on a number of the charts. Be especially careful not to take these readings too seriously if they were computed on a limited number of history years (most often the case when readings are this high or low). The more years used in the analysis, the more meaningful and reliable the readings are.

The weekly percentage reading and how it relates to current time. The weekly readings have been obtained by aligning contract data, from last trading day to first trading day. The month and week readings, listed along the bottom of each chart, may not necessarily apply to every market year. They are only reference points. In future years or past years, there may be several weeks' shift in timing.

In such cases you can calculate the correct week and month by working backward from the last entry (lower right-hand part of the chart), and counting the week numbers to current time. This is not a difficult task. Simply determine from exchange rules when the contracts are scheduled to expire. Make your determinations of the appropriate week and month for this year accordingly. After some practice, you will be able to isolate the time frame rather easily.

In studying actual market behavior, you will gain additional experience, which may be helpful in determining if the seasonals have shifted this year compared to the norm. It is important to determine to the best of your ability if there has been a shift in the current year. I issue updates of this study every year, and I suggest you keep up to date. In so doing you will always have the most up-to-date version of the charts, which will help you make your determination of the actual weekly readings considerably easier.

LIMIT YOUR LOSSES REGARDLESS OF WHAT THE SEASONALS SAY!

One of the worst errors a trader can make is to become totally dependent on one method or technique. We do not yet have totally reliable seasonal trading tools. Use good sense when making trades. Use stop losses; limit risk.

WHAT YOU SHOULD KNOW ABOUT STATISTICAL RELIABILITY AND SEASONAL SPREAD CHARTS

The study of statistics is primarily concerned with such issues as determining whether given events are random or chance occurrences or if they are predictable events that are a function of some underlying causal or correlational factor. The more observations you make of a particular event, the more information you will have regarding the repetitive or random nature of that event.

In the case of a coin toss, for example, the outcome of each toss is independent of the outcome of previous tosses, assuming an unbiased coin. Therefore, even if you have tossed 10 successive heads, there is no guarantee that the next toss will be a head or a tail. Assuming that the coin is not improperly weighted or intentionally designed to show a preference, the results of each toss are purely random.

Certain events, however, are not random; they do in fact show repetitive patterns. But it is impossible to know exactly how repetitive they are until we closely examine them mathematically. In order to do so, we need considerable data. This poses an interesting problem for the futures market inasmuch as there are only limited data available in many of the markets. In the meat and livestock markets, for example, futures trading began in the mid-1960s. In the grain and soybean complex, there are considerable data as far back as the late 1800s; however, trading volume was very thin in some years, contract months differ somewhat from current standards, and daily price ranges were very small in many cases. In the financials, such as T-bonds and some currency futures, the historical data are limited, although cash data are available.

Clearly the issue is to test as much valid data as we have, devise a different type of test, or not use the data at all. Not to use the data for assistance in making trading decisions is out of the question. To use and test the available data is the only alternative. Although not everyone will be pleased with the limitations of this study, I nevertheless have chosen the only viable alternative of the few available choices.

Remember that there are distinct statistical limitations to this study, and you must therefore use the results with these limitations clearly in mind. Until more statistically reliable methods are developed, we must employ what we have with the appropriate degree of caution and continue to study the actual seasonal trends to see how closely they conform to previous seasonal analyses and expectations.

Ultimately, the test of reality is the final test of any seasonal tendency. Because there are no hard and fast rules for using seasonal tendencies in spreads or flat positions (i.e., a simple long or short position), I encourage you to experiment with your own applications. The key, of course, is observation. By studying history and observing relationships, you will learn more about the markets than any book, trading course, or seminar can teach you.

EXAMPLES OF SEASONAL SPREAD APPLICATIONS

There are various applications of seasonal spread tendencies. Here are a few examples of how the information might be used.

High-Probability Seasonal Run

Consider the use of a high-probability seasonal run in order to determine a potential spreading opportunity. Remember that these periods are marked with arrows up or down. The more consecutive or nearly consecutive arrows are up or down in a weekly run, the more likely it is to represent a reliable seasonal move. To use the seasonal runs effectively, first find the period of seasonal run that interests you.

A good way to spot seasonal runs is to look for a succession of up or down arrows on the composite charts and a bold line plot. Assume that you have isolated a high-probability seasonal run in the March soybeans versus March corn spread. You will note from the seasonal composite spread chart (see Figure 5-6) that from mid-September through mid-October, this spread moves down. In other words, March soybeans loses to March wheat. This means that on or about the middle of September (Week 23), you would want to enter the spread, selling short buying March wheat.

You would remain in this spread until you are either stopped out if the spread moves against you by a predetermined stop-loss amount or exit when the seasonal down run is over. Because the spread can continue to move in your favor beyond the ideal exit date, you could remain in the spread, following it up with a mental trailing stop loss. See Figure 5-3 for an illustration of a reliable seasonal. Such spreads may be among the riskiest of all, so exercise caution.

High-Reliability Weekly Runs

Many of the seasonal spread composite charts show a span of several weeks of high-reliability percentage readings. These periods of seasonal runs are typically a good time for high-probability seasonal trends. The following weekly readings are an example of such a seasonal run: 59%, 75%, 68%, 67%, 78%, 69%, 61%, 69%, 79%.

Seasonal Spreads and Timing

Consider the use of timing indicators in conjunction with seasonal spreads. Here is the recommended procedure:

1. Determine the spread you want to trade by studying the composite spread charts.
2. Examine the spread for the current year. If the actual trend this year is essentially similar to the composite seasonal trend, then you can reasonably assume that the spread is behaving in a normal seasonal fashion and the spread is acceptable for trading

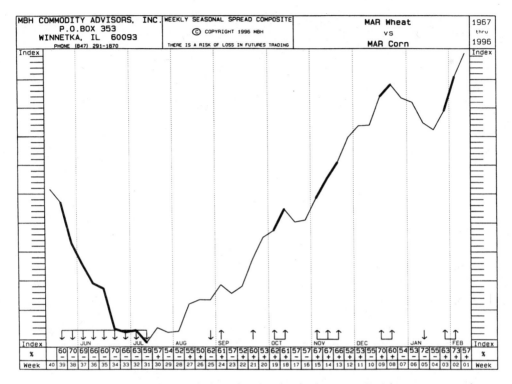

Figure 5-3 Seasonal spread chart for March wheat versus March corn seasonal run, 1967–1996. Note Weeks 39 through 31. (Copyright © 1996 by MBH Commodity Advisors, Inc.)

this year. A spread that is not acting reasonably in line with its composite might be rejected on the basis of its deviation from its average seasonal trend.

3. As the ideal entry time approaches, you can enter the spread by the ideal entry date or by using various timing indicators such as a 9-day or 18-day moving average, or 28-day rate of change or momentum.

Using Intraday Charts to Pinpoint Spread Timing

Another approach to improving spread entry and exit is to use intraday charts and timing indicators. Consider the following example:

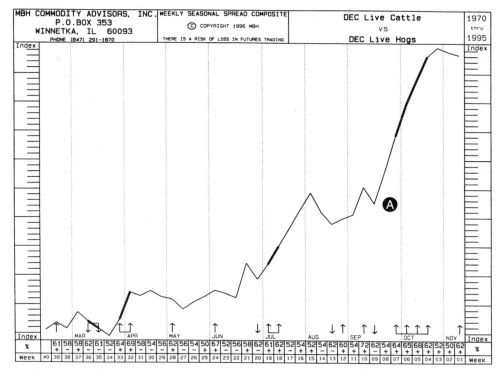

Figure 5-4   Seasonal spread composite chart for December live cattle versus December live hogs, 1970–1995. Point A marks a seasonal low. (Copyright © 1996 by MBH Commodity Advisors, Inc.)

You have decided to enter the long December cattle versus short December hog spread based on an anticipated seasonal upmove that tends to begin in late September and tends to end in mid- to late October. Figure 5-4 shows the weekly seasonal composite with the indicated period noted by the bold plot line.

Now consult a daily or intraday chart of this spread. The chart can be daily, hourly, half-hourly, or even less depending on your time frame. If you are a short-term trader, you'll want to use an intraday chart of shorter duration. The hourly chart for the spread this year is shown in Figure 5-5. As you can see from it, the spread started topping

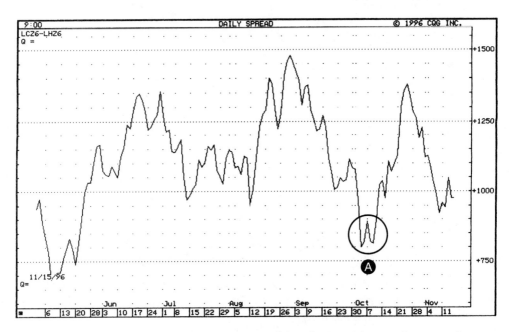

Figure 5-5 Hourly chart showing seasonal low in December cattle versus December hogs. Point A marks a seasonal low. Note how the actual move developed as shown in Figure 5-4. (Copyright © 1996 by CQG, Inc. Reprinted with permission.)

on schedule. The spread consolidated at point A and moved in the anticipated direction after that. The expected recovery (cattle gaining on hogs) is now forming a base from which the ideal seasonal may begin.

An hourly chart at point A could have helped you to pinpoint the start of this seasonal move.

Figure 5-6 shows another illustration. The seasonal move down, in March soybeans versus March wheat, is illustrated with an hourly chart and an 18-period moving average indicator to time entry and exit.

Figures 5-7 through 5-12 show more examples.

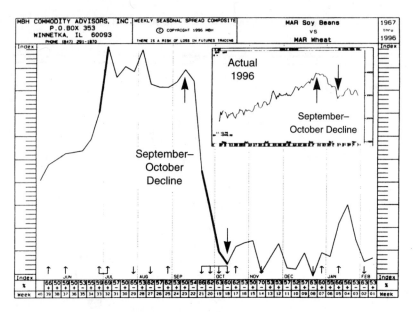

Figure 5-6 Seasonal spread chart for March soybeans versus March wheat, 1967–1996, showing seasonal run ideal entry and exit. (Copyright © 1996 by MBH Commodity Advisors, Inc.)

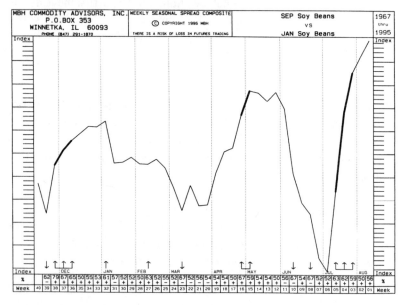

Figure 5-7 Seasonal spread chart for September soybeans versus January soybeans, 1967–1995. (Copyright © 1996 by MBH Commodity Advisors, Inc.)

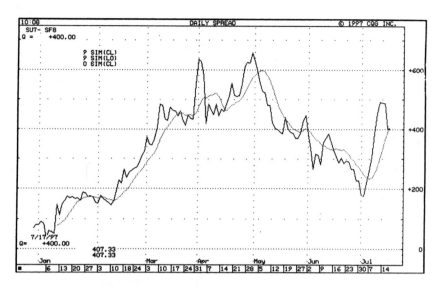

Figure 5-8 Seasonal spread chart for September soybeans versus January soybeans daily spread chart. (Copyright © 1997 by CQG, Inc. Reprinted with permission.)

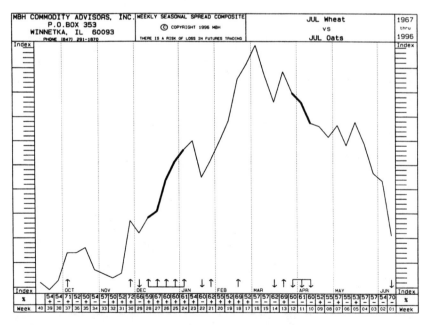

Figure 5-9 Seasonal spread chart for July wheat versus July oats, 1967–1996. (Copyright © 1996 by MBH Commodity Advisors, Inc.)

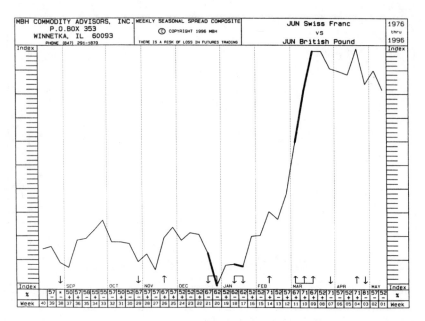

Figure 5-10 Seasonal spread chart for June Swiss franc versus June British pound, 1976–1996. (Copyright © 1996 by MBH Commodity Advisors, Inc.)

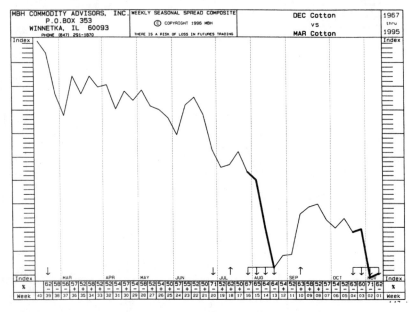

Figure 5-11 Seasonal spread chart for December cotton versus March cotton, 1967–1995. (Copyright © 1996 by MBH Commodity Advisors, Inc.)

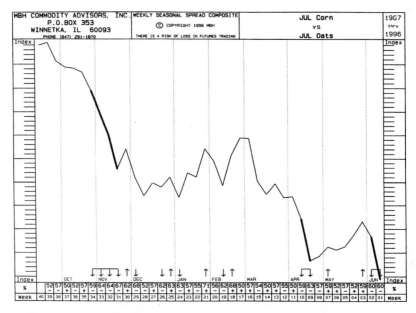

Figure 5-12   Seasonal spread chart for July corn versus July oats, 1967–1996. (Copyright © 1996 by MBH Commodity Advisors, Inc.)

6

DAILY SEASONAL
PRICE TENDENCIES

We know that seasonal price patterns exist not only on a weekly and monthly basis, but on a daily basis as well. Considerable historical research has shown that there are given calendar days of the year when there exists a high probability of price movement in a given direction. Naturally, determining seasonality must be related to statistical validity. The longer the historical database is, the greater your confidence will be in your seasonal observations. A price tendency that has occurred 80 percent of the time during the past 5 years is relatively meaningless when compared to a price tendency that has occurred 80 percent of the time during the past 25 years or more.

A variety of statistical techniques can be performed on raw data in order to ascertain the degree of confidence you should have in the conclusions you derive from seasonal computations. My work with seasonality has taught me that there are many popular myths about seasonal tendencies, which are perpetuated not as a function of historical reality but as a function of popular belief. A good case in point is the May versus November soybean spread. The composite seasonal tendency (see Figure 6-1) clearly suggests that more often than not, the general trend has been as represented by the composite seasonal charts. On

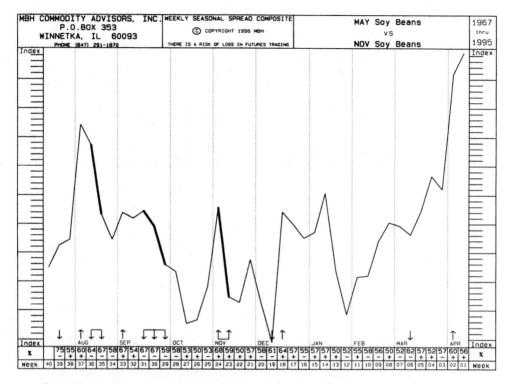

Figure 6-1 May versus November soybean spread, 1967–1995. (Copyright © 1996 by MBH Commodity Advisors, Inc.)

several occasions in the 1970s and 1980s, the spread made large and dramatic price moves favoring May soybeans. This is what accounts for the upward slope of the chart. In addition, the historically low margin requirements for this spread and the subsequent potential for large percentage return on initial margin helped create a large following for this spread. The May versus November soybean spread remains, even now, one of the most widely followed spreads in the futures industry. What is interesting and discernable only from analyzing the seasonals is that the May versus November soybean spread has only a mediocre record of historical reliability and is not an especially good spread in terms of consistency.

TABLE 6-1 Merrill's Pre- and Postholiday Behavior: Percentage of Years in Which the Dow-Jones Industrial Average Posted an Increase for the Day

Holiday	Day Before	Day After
Washington's Birthday	45.8	40.2
Good Friday	60.9	46.5
Memorial Day	74.1	42.3
Independence Day	76.7	59.8
Labor Day	81.2	57.0
Thanksgiving	56.6	65.9
Christmas	72.4	52.9
New Year's Day	72.1	52.9
Total all holidays	68.1	52.2

Source: Data from A. Merrill, *The Behavior of Prices on Wall Street* (Chappaqua, N.Y.: Analysis Press, 1984), p. 14.

We must avoid dealing in seasonal myths or expectations lest we begin to expect the occurrence of certain events that in fact are not justifiable historically. The same is true of daily seasonal price tendencies. For years, many traders have expected certain things to occur on given days or within a group of days. Traders speak of such things as "pre-Fourth of July meat rallies" or "pre-Christmas demand." The best way to determine whether commodity folklore is actually fact is to test the expectations.

"Daily" seasonality is not unique to commodity prices. Arthur A. Merrill in his classic book, *The Behavior of Prices on Wall Street* (Chappaqua, N.Y.: Analysis Press, 1984), provided specific examples of stock market price behavior prior to major holidays. For example, Merrill showed clearly that prices for the Dow-Jones Industrial Average exhibited highly reliable price tendencies the day before legal and religious holidays. Table 6-1 shows some of the relationships he discovered using statistics from January 1897 through December 1983. Merrill used a sufficiently large data sample to constitute a valid statistical test of his price tendencies.

DAYS-TO-CONTRACT EXPIRATION METHOD

Recall from my explanation of the technique for computing weekly seasonal price tendencies that the procedure involved placing data into an array form based on calendar dates. A monthly seasonal tendency can be determined by comparing prices on a monthly basis across a period of many years. In other words, in calculating a monthly seasonal composite, one compares all of the similar months in the database, arriving at a seasonal tendency direction and percentage for each month. Some seasonal analysts have proposed alternative methods for determining seasonals—ones not based on comparison of dates, weeks, or months based on the calendar but rather on other seasonal variables.

This is a cogent approach and should be investigated further. Sheldon Knight has compared his results in seasonal analysis using exact calendar dates for seasonal trade entry and exit with the use of other time-based entry and exit, such as holidays and first notice days.[1] Based on a relatively small sample, Knight concluded that his suggested alternatives to exact calendar date entry and exit were superior to the other methods. But his data sample was exceptionally small, and his conclusions cannot be taken as anything more than a worthwhile direction for further research.

In calculating daily seasonal price tendencies, the simplest procedure is to compare calendar days because people tend to think in terms of dates and act accordingly based on their thoughts and perceptions. For example, the market is always closed on the Fourth of July, Memorial Day, and Christmas Day. Certain attitudes tend to prevail just prior to and after important calendar dates. Therefore, the preferable procedure is to present the raw data on a month and calendar day basis. For example, every July 1 would be compared with every other July 1 during the entire database. It is possible that during certain years, July 1 will fall on a day when the market is closed. Should this occur, the day is dropped from the database and calculations are made on the available data only.

[1]Sheldon Knight, "Trading the Seasonal Time Line," *Futures* (April 1997).

ALTERNATE SEASONAL COMPUTATIONS

Another technique by which daily seasonal tendencies can be calculated is to place the data in an array form based not on calendar date but rather in terms of contract expiration date. Most futures contracts expire on or about the same date. Through the years, there have been some differences, and so this type of manipulation may not truly result in a clear perception of daily seasonal price tendencies. In order to understand why, you must first understand how the data are handled.

Assume that the last day of trading for July live hog futures is July 18. This technique uses the data for different years and makes the last day of trading the beginning point of the data, regardless of calendar date. The program then works backward to the starting point in order to find where there is overlap among all the contracts. This is done because not all futures contracts for the same commodity and month begin trading on exactly the same day. What we have, then, is a string of data theoretically encompassing almost exactly the same number of trading days within which, however, the exact calendar dates are not necessarily lined up for comparison. The logic behind this analysis is that seasonality is being measured as a function of days prior to contract expiration.

Since futures traders do not often think in this fashion, I regard the calendar date comparison as much more realistic and have used it exclusively in my daily seasonal work. For those who wish to take the time to apply the alternate method, there may be some benefits. However, I think that the benefits will be rather limited and that we may, in fact, not actually be testing seasonality.

OVERVIEW OF THE TECHNIQUE

The technique is quite simple. An array is constructed during which all similar calendar dates are lined up in a stacked fashion year to year. (See Figure 6-2.) Thereafter, various comparative techniques are applied, and decisions regarding normalizing and so forth are made prior to final manipulation of the data. This technique is the simplest in terms of computer applications.

DAILY SEASONAL PRICE TENDENCIES

Jan-69	26	29	31	34	37	41	37	35	36	33	32	31	33	35	37	38	39	41	44	45	47
Jan-70	45	47	49	51	55	57	51	49	47	48	55	56	57	55	56	55	54	54	53	52	31
Jan-71	30	34	35	46	45	44	45	43	42	43	47	46	48	49	50	51	54	53	56	56	58
Jan-72	49	48	47	45	49	51	55	58	69	65	67	62	60	64	70	67	71	78	76	69	63
Jan-73	71	77	78	76	75	78	79	80	81	86	87	89	88	86	85	86	78	79	80	82	84
Jan-74	87	79	71	77	78	78	77	76	78	79	80	81	82	83	87	89	90	88	87	89	77
Jan-75	Etc	Etc	Etc	Etc	Etc	Etc	Etc	Etc	Etc	Etc	Etc	Etc	Etc	Etc	Etc	Etc	Etc	Etc	Etc	Etc	Etc
Jan-76																					
Jan-77																					
Jan-78																					
Jan-79																					
Jan-80																					
Jan-81																					
Jan-82																					
Jan-83																					
Jan-84																					
Jan-85																					
Jan-86																					
Jan-87																					
Jan-88																					
Jan-89																					
Jan-90																					
Jan-91																					
Jan-92																					
Jan-93																					
Jan-94																					
Jan-95																					
Jan-96																					
Jan-97																					
Totals	%																				

Figure 6-2   Seasonal data—raw calculation array.

The output appears in final form as illustrated in Figure 6-3. A seasonal reading can be obtained for every calendar day of the year with the understanding that during certain years, the markets will be closed on some calendar days, whereas they will be open on the same calendar days during other years.

Examine Figure 6-4. Remember that these readings do not forecast what prices will do; they merely show what prices have done on a given calendar day over the period of time examined. Figures 6-5 through 6-9 show a number of daily seasonal analyses.

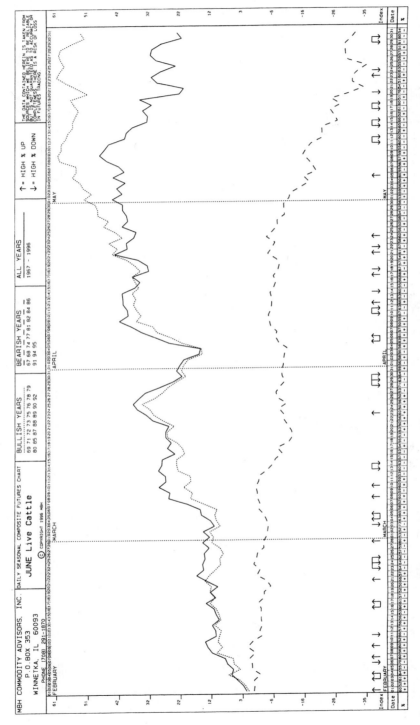

Figure 6-3 Daily seasonal tendencies in June live cattle, 1967–1996. (Copyright © 1996 by MBH Commodity Advisors, Inc.)

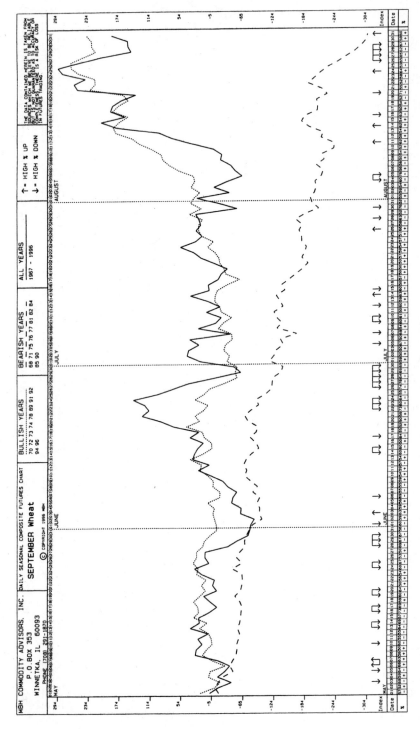

Figure 6-4 Daily seasonal tendencies in September wheat, 1967–1996. (Copyright © 1996 by MBH Commodity Advisors, Inc.)

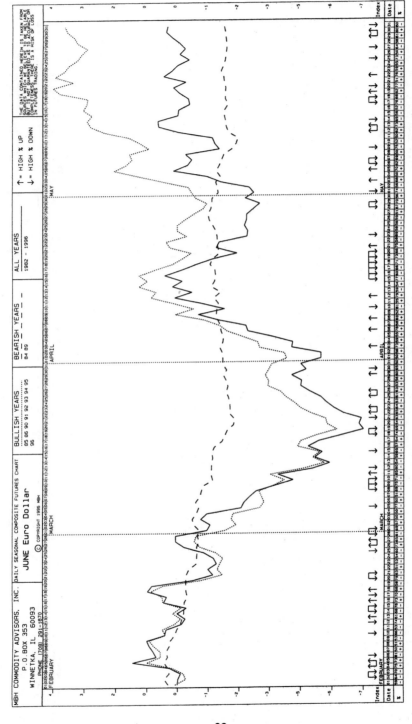

Figure 6-5 Daily seasonal tendencies in June Eurodollar, 1982–1996. (Copyright © 1996 by MBH Commodity Advisors, Inc.)

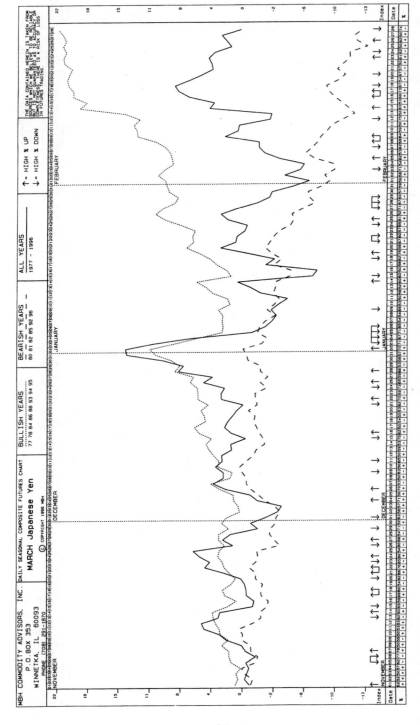

Figure 6-6 Daily seasonal tendencies in March Japanese yen, 1977–1996. (Copyright © 1996 by MBH Commodity Advisors, Inc.)

94

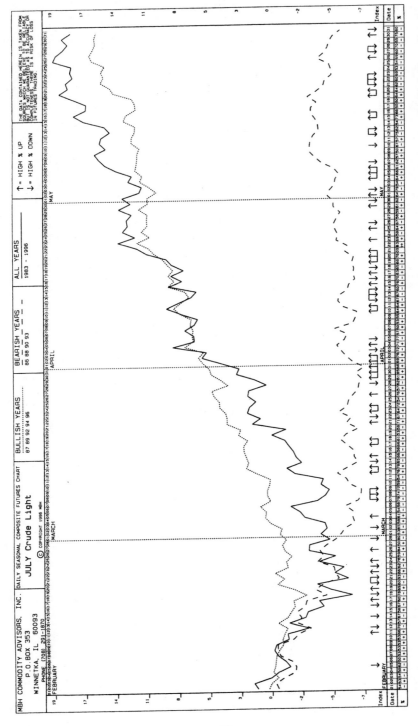

Figure 6-7 Daily seasonal tendencies in July crude light, 1983–1996. (Copyright © 1996 by MBH Commodity Advisors, Inc.)

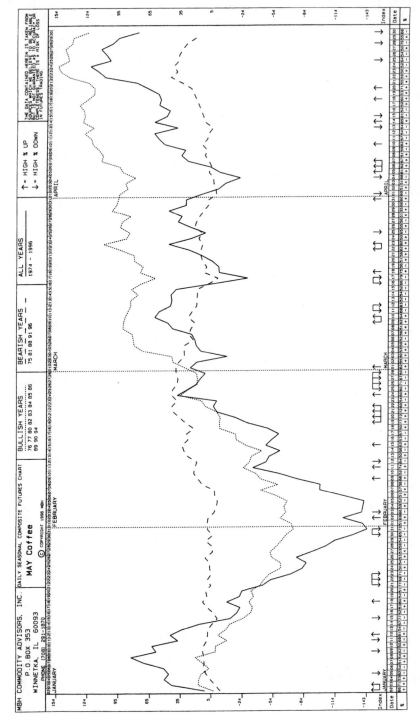

Figure 6-8 Daily seasonal tendencies in May coffee, 1974–1996. (Copyright © 1996 by MBH Commodity Advisors, Inc.)

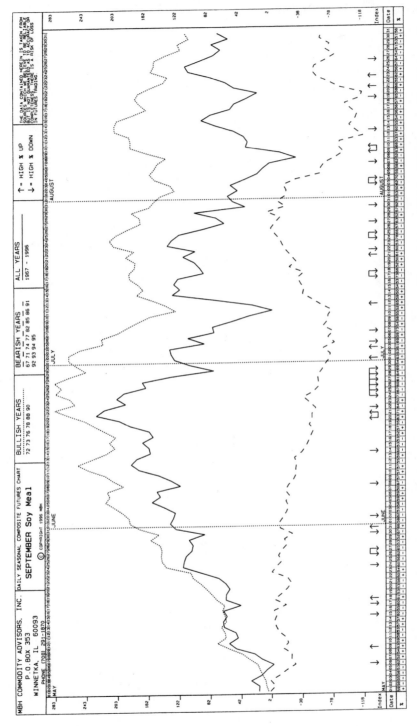

Figure 6-9 Daily seasonal tendencies in September soybean meal, 1967–1996. (Copyright © 1996 by MBH Commodity Advisors, Inc.)

7

CRITICAL SEASONAL MONTH CONCEPT

One of the most important seasonal indicators is what I have termed the *critical month indicator* (CMI). CMI is based on the idea that certain months offer support and resistance that, if penetrated, often lead to a significant move in the direction of the penetration. CMI is therefore based on two concepts, both of which are very important in the markets: time and price.

Yale Hirsch and Art Merrill, prolific researchers in the area of stocks and the stock market, have written extensively about market patterns, some of which are similar to the CMI. Two of the very best books money can buy are Yale Hirsch's *Don't Sell Stocks on Monday* (New York: Facts on File, 1986) and Art Merrill's *The Behavior of Prices on Wall Street* (New York: Analysis Press, 1984). If you haven't read these classics, you're missing out on some powerful concepts that can make you money. Don't wait any longer to read them!

HOW THE CMI IS DETERMINED

Virtually any month of the year can be a critical month; however, some months are more critically important than others are. In most markets,

January is a critical month (CM), as is December. The usual month of the seasonal high or low is often a critical month in specific markets. In wheat, therefore, May through July are CMs since seasonal lows often occur in this time window. January and February are CMs as well, since highs usually come in this time frame.

There are no hard and fast rules about determining which months of the year will be critical. However, most months can be used as CMs if you follow the CM timing rules:

1. *Determine the month you will be using as the CM.* Assume for the sake of illustration that you have selected December.

2. *Wait until the CM has come to an end.* In other words, wait until December ends. Once the month has ended find the extreme high and extreme low for the entire month. This means the highest of the high prices (intraday) and the lowest of the low prices.

Let's say that you selected July corn, with December as the CM. Assume that the highest high for December is 2.35 and the lowest low for December is 2.21. These two points will become your CMI buy point (CMIB) and your CMI sell point (CMIS).

Watch weekly closing prices for a weekly close above the CMIB or below the CMIS. The penetration of the CMIS or CMIB must be on a weekly closing basis. In other words, the CMIS and/or CMIB may be penetrated during the week. This doesn't count. The penetration *must* occur on a closing basis for the entire week (the closing price on the last trading day of the week).

3. *Make your decision.* Assume that in this case, July corn closed at 2.38, above the CMIB. You would buy it using either a dollar risk management stop loss or a reversing signal below the CMIS.

The CMI is specific to each market. You wouldn't use a CMI signal in corn for the purpose of trading oats, or wheat, or beans, or anything else.

That's all there is to the CMI. It's that simple—and that complicated.

CHARACTERISTICS OF THE CMI

A penetration of the CMI often results in a big move consistent with the direction of the penetration. Some of the biggest up- and down-moves have occurred following a CMIB or CMIS signal. Yes, there is always risk; however, the big moves are often those that require bigger risks.

The sooner a CMI occurs after the end of the CM, the more likely the move is to be a big one. Therefore, I suggest you closely watch the markets in January for penetration of the December CMIB and CMIS points.

EXAMPLES OF CMI HISTORY

Copper Futures

One of the best CMI signals has occurred in copper futures. Penetration of the December and/or January highs or lows has often been a trigger for some of the largest moves in copper history. Some time ago, I listed the December CMI signals in copper all the way back to the 1950s on a year-by-year basis, along with my analysis of the signals. The commentary discussed each and every CMI since then. It was very clear that the CMI had been an outstanding indicator of major bull moves in copper prices. Bear moves were predictable as well, but the bull moves clearly had an upper hand in terms of their frequency and magnitude:

1949: December low penetrated, followed by persistent drop in prices through June.

1950: December low penetrated, followed by minor drop; then December high penetrated, followed by 100 percent rally!

1951: Trading suspended.

1952: Trading suspended.

1953: Trading suspended through June.

1954: December low penetration followed by minor drop, and then December high penetration followed by big rally.

1955: December high penetrated, resulting in rally from about 34 to over 52 several months later.

1956: A "double-whammy" year. Penetration of December high resulted in a big rally. Second penetration of December low resulted in a drop from about 46 to about 33.

1957: Another winner! Penetration of December low brought immediate bear market from 32 to 24.

1958:   December low penetration brought minor decline, but penetration of December high brought rally from 25 to 32.

1959:   Immediate rally when December high was penetrated. Thereafter, other CMs took precedence.

1960:   Bear market, but a minor one, followed penetration of December low.

1961:   Minor bear move after December low was penetrated, followed by strong rally from about 26 to 33.

1962:   CM did not work this year with any significant follow-through on penetration of December high and low.

1963:   Very small range this year, but penetration of December high did get some follow-through on upside.

1964:   A classic! The market blasted off when December high was penetrated—rallied from about 32 to 62!

1965:   One of those rare years in which the December high or low CMI signal did not develop.

1966:   Classic rally. Moved from about 62 to 83 after penetrating the December high.

1967:   Good drop after penetration of December low. Fell from about 50 to a low of 42.

1968:   Penetration of the December high brought a rally followed by a drop below the December low and a bear move through midyear.

1969:   A great rally followed penetration of the December high. The market moved from about 53 to over 76.

1970:   Penetration of the December low and then high resulted in small moves, but the second penetration of the December low resulted in a big drop. The January CM worked much better.

1971:   January worked better again, but the December CMI was not bad. Small loss on December low penetration. Small profit after December high penetration.

1972:   Similar to the previous year. Very small range compared to the last few years.

1973:   The best one to date! Moved from about 51 to 110 after penetration of the December high.

1974: Small decline followed December low penetration, but major rally after December high penetration.

1975: Basically a whipsaw year, but signals were not bad. Small loss on December low penetration. Small profit after December high penetration.

1976: Good rally after penetration of December high.

1977: Another winner! Two signals this year—a buy followed by a sell.

1978: Small decline after December low penetration. Good rally after December high penetration.

1979: Great rally followed penetration of the December high. Moved from about 72 to about 98 quickly.

1980: Major rally followed move through December high, but it was a quick one. A bear market followed.

1981: Drop below December low resulted in move from approximately 78 to 70 by year end.

1982: Penetration of December low was followed by a drop from about 72 to a low of 53 by midyear.

1983: December high penetration resulted in a small rally.

1984: Small range this year with minor penetrations, resulting in small moves on both sides of the CM.

1985: Also a narrow-range year—no major CM moves this year.

1986: Also a narrow-range year, with small moves on both sides of the CM.

1987: A classic move following penetration of the December high. Moved from 62 to near 140—the biggest move ever.

1988: A decline followed penetration of the December low, but this was a highly volatile year with better CM signals later in the year.

1989: Close below December low triggered drop from about 143 to 100 in rather short order.

1990: No follow-through after move below December low; small rally after move over December high.

1991: Basically a sideways year with little follow-through on sell side of the CM breakout.

1992: Close above December high brought a rally from about 103 to a high of 116 and over.

1993: The December low was penetrated, and a drop from 9500 to the recent low of 7200 was the result.

1994: The December high was penetrated, giving a CM buy signal. A rally from about 85 to over 115 then developed.

1995: The December high penetration resulted in an eventual rally from about 130 to 145+; however, it was not a straight up move.

1996: Two CMI signals developed. The sell signal developed first with minimal follow-through. A buy signal later developed, also with minimal follow-through. Both CMI signals would have lost money unless a stop-loss had been used.

The December CMI has been a very powerful indicator in copper, which all traders should study and use.

CMI History of Gold Futures

The following list of CMI breakouts in gold above the January high and low also provides an interesting analysis.

1973: The market rallied strong from its breakout point, moving from about 65 to a high of over 125 by midyear.

1974: Another strong rally followed the January high breakout at about 142 to a high of 200 by year-end.

1975: The high penetration came first but was reversed. A small loss followed, then the low was penetrated as the price moved considerably lower by year-end.

1976: This was also a bearish year. The low was penetrated after January was over, and a bear move followed.

1977: A CM high buy signal developed, taking prices from about 134 to a high of over 160 by year-end.

1978: Another bullish move: a CM buy signal at about 165 with a move to about 245 by year-end.

1979: A major bull move following a penetration at about 240 followed by a rally to near 650!

1980: A major bear move after a CM sell signal. Price dropped from about 610 to near 455 before rallying.

1981: Another major drop after a CM sell as prices dropped from about 450 to under 400.

1982: Another bear move following penetration of the CM sell point, followed by a strong rally above the CM buy.

1983: A major decline followed penetration of the January low CM sell point.

1984: The market fell sharply this year as well after the CM sell point was penetrated.

1985: Prices moved higher after the CM buy signal. A major bull move developed.

1986: This was a bullish year as well. Close above the CM resistance of about 360 brought a move to over 440.

1987: Another bullish move came this year after a CM buy signal.

1988: The market dropped sharply following a CM sell signal.

1989: The CM sell brought a decline and then a rally.

1990: Although a strong rally developed, prices did not penetrate the CM buy point after first giving a sell.

1991: Slow and steady erosion followed a CM sell signal as prices declined most of the year.

1992: Another year of slow and steady erosion following a CM sell signal.

1993: The market rallied strong after giving a CM buy signal early in the year.

1994: A CM buy signal resulted in only minimal follow-through.

1995: A CM buy signal resulted in minimal upmove.

1996: A CM buy signal lost money; however, a CM sell in April would have been profitable.

MARKETS TO WATCH FOR CMI SIGNALS

December and January are the most important months of the year for CMI signals, particularly on the buy side and particularly in the following markets and contract months:

- *Meats.* June cattle and hogs, May bellies, and April feeder cattle.
- *Grains.* July soybean complex, July wheat, July corn, December corn (May CMI).
- *Metals.* June gold, July silver, July copper, April platinum. In these markets, a weekly close below the December or January low can lead to big bear markets. Many of the tops in gold and silver have been made early in the new year.
- *Tropicals.* Coffee and cocoa: July and December.

IN CONCLUSION

The CMI is a valuable indicator for catching bigger moves. You can do your own CMI research with just a little data history and a spreadsheet program. It will be time well spent, particularly if you like to catch larger moves. Although it is by no means perfect, it has had a lengthy history of success, often catching big yearly moves early in their inception. Examine the sample CMI charts in Figures 7-1 and 7-2.

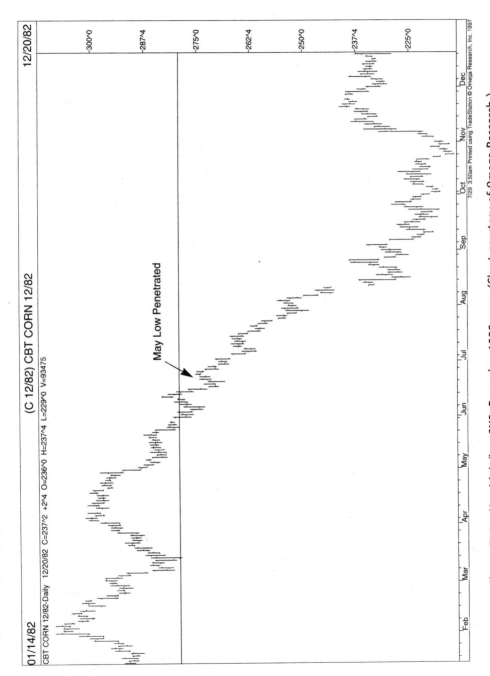

Figure 7-1 May high/low CMI, December 1982 corn. (Chart courtesy of Omega Research.)

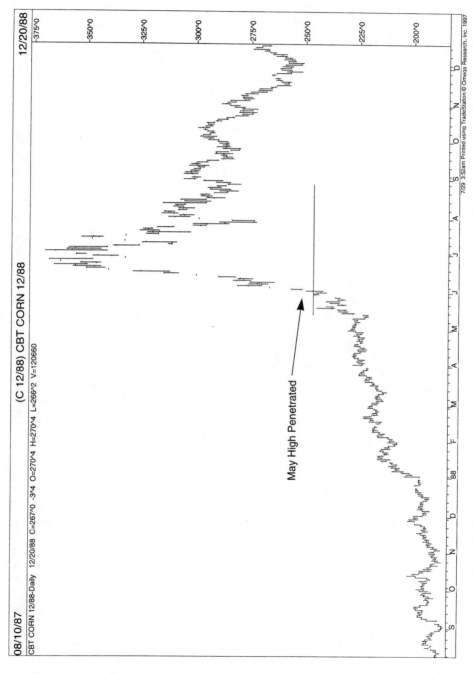

Figure 7-2 May high/low CMI, December 1988 corn. (Chart courtesy of Omega Research.)

8

KEY DATE SEASONALS

A variation on the daily and weekly seasonal computations is the concept of key date seasonals, which are similar to the concept of seasonal run, described in Chapter 6. The difference is that the seasonal run encompasses weekly seasonal readings over a period of three weeks or more during which percentage reliability readings tend to be high. The same technique is now refined and applied on a calendar-day basis in order to optimize timing.

METHOD OF COMPUTATION

Computation of key date seasonals is a laborious process that should be done by computer. In effect, the computer is instructed to make calculations on a loop based on hypothetical buying and selling during specific calendar days over a lengthy data history.

Let's assume that we are attempting to find key date seasonals in gold futures. The first step is to place all the data in an array by calendar day. The second step is to instruct the computer to make a hypothetical purchase or sale on the closing price of a given date and then to liquidate the position on the next day.

The computer calculates the hypothetical profit or loss had this trade been made from the closing price of Day 1 to the closing price of

Day 2 every year in the database. The computer is then instructed to institute a hypothetical buy or sell position on Day 1 and then to close out the position on Day 3. The same calculation of hypothetical profit or loss is done. The computer is then instructed to begin again with Day 1 and go to Day 4 in the database. (The day numbers are, of course, specific calendar dates.) The process therefore proceeds in an $n + 1$ fashion until the end of the database has been reached. The computer is then instructed to begin with Day 2 of the database, again proceeding on an $n + 1$ fashion until the nth or last price has been reached in the database.

The data can be presented in array form similar to correlation coefficients, which are produced as a function of factor analytic techniques. The data can also be presented in a simpler format, as shown in Table 8-1. Further instructions can be issued to the computer to print only those key seasonal entry-exit time spans that have shown an average profit above a given amount and a percentage occurrence above a given amount. The result is a series of key date seasonals trades, which can be refined by adding money management aspects in order to limit losses and maximize profits.

One technique of refining the key date seasonal output is by adding to the program a hypothetical risk point or stop loss for each of the key date seasonal trades. By varying the risk point, you can determine the maximum percentage move contrary to the entry price that has occurred during the history of the given key date time span. Table 8-2 shows a key date seasonal trade computed with several different percentage stop-loss figures and the corresponding hypothetical results. You can see that variation of the stop can produce significantly different results.

Application of key date seasonal trades is a relatively simple matter. The performance of key date seasonal trades as well as the performance of weekly seasonals and daily seasonals themselves can be markedly improved through the use of money management techniques, accumulation techniques, and filtering with timing signals, cycles, moving averages, and price chart patterns.

Tables 8-3 through 8-6 contain a number of key date seasonals which I have isolated as examples as to what can be achieved through the use of this strategy. Remember that no seasonal technique or, for that matter, trading methodology is infallible. Just because a key date seasonal has been profitable a high percentage of the time in past years

TABLE 8-1 Key Date Seasonal Trade in Long June Live Hogs (Enter: 12/30; Exit: 1/6; Stop: 3; P/L Ratio: 13.94)

Year	Date In	Price In	Date Out	Price Out	Profit/Loss	Total
1970	12/30/69	26.750	1/6/70	27.620	0.870	0.870
1971	12/30/70	17.850	1/6/71	17.950	0.100	0.970
1972	12/30/71	26.700	1/6/72	27.200	0.500	1.470
1973	1/2/72	29.620	1/8/73	30.250	0.630	2.100
1974	12/31/73	45.320	1/7/74	49.570	4.250	6.350
1975	12/30/74	43.670	1/6/75	44.650	0.980	7.330
1976	12/30/75	43.850	1/6/76	46.650	2.800	10.130
1977	12/30/76	37.320	1/6/77	36.870	−0.450	9.680
1978	12/30/77	40.950	1/6/78	42.070	1.120	10.800
1979	1/2/78	47.670	1/8/79	48.200	0.530	11.330
1980	12/31/79	43.970	1/7/80	43.950	−0.020	11.310
1981	12/30/80	53.520	1/6/81	53.720	0.200	11.510
1982	12/30/81	45.770	1/6/82	47.170	1.400	12.910
1983	12/30/82	54.750	1/6/83	55.770	1.020	13.930
1984	12/30/83	53.050	1/6/84	54.170	1.120	15.050
1985	12/31/84	54.570	1/7/85	54.050	−0.520	14.530
1986	12/30/85	45.470	1/6/86	45.300	−0.170	14.360
1987	12/30/86	46.050	1/6/87	46.520	0.470	14.830
1988	12/30/87	41.970	1/6/88	43.900	1.930	16.760
1989	12/30/88	49.570	1/6/89	49.870	0.300	17.060
1990	1/2/89	48.550	1/8/90	52.470	3.920	20.980
1991	12/31/90	51.370	1/7/91	53.220	1.850	22.830
1992	12/30/91	42.600	1/6/92	43.770	1.170	24.000
1993	12/30/92	46.850	1/6/93	47.000	0.150	24.150
1994	12/30/93	52.170	1/6/94	53.970	1.800	25.950
1995	12/30/94	45.170	1/6/95	44.220	−0.950	25.000
1996	1/2/95	51.700	1/8/96	51.750	0.050	25.050
1997	12/30/96	77.220	1/6/97	79.470	2.250	27.300

Trades: 28	Average Profit: 1.28
Winners: 23	Average Loss: −0.42
Losers: 5	% Average Profit: 2.80
% Winners: 82.14	% Average Loss: −0.94

Note: There is a risk of loss in futures trading.

**TABLE 8-2   Key Date Seasonal Trade in Short March Silver
(Enter: 11/5; Exit: 11/27; Stop: 5; P/L Ratio: 4.69)**

Year	Date In	Price In	Date Out	Price Out	Profit/Loss	Total
1973	11/6/72	188.200	11/27/72	183.200	5.000	5.000
1974	11/5/73	298.200	11/27/73	288.200	10.000	15.000
1975	11/6/74	515.200	11/27/74	463.300	51.900	66.900
1976	11/5/75	451.800	11/28/75	418.600	33.200	100.100
1977	11/5/76	443.500	11/29/76	434.400	9.100	109.200
1978	11/7/77	500.900	11/28/77	481.600	19.300	128.500
1979	11/6/78	597.500	11/27/78	613.500	−16.000	112.500
1980	11/5/79	1,705.500	11/27/79	1,747.000	−41.500	71.000
1981	11/5/80	1,998.000	11/28/80	1,945.000	53.000	124.000
1982	11/5/81	957.500	11/27/81	856.700	100.800	224.800
1983	11/5/82	1,086.000	11/29/82	990.000	96.000	320.800
1984	11/7/83	929.800	11/28/83	932.000	−2.200	318.600
1985	11/5/84	791.900	11/27/84	728.400	63.500	382.100
1986	11/5/85	624.800	11/27/85	622.000	2.800	384.900
1987	11/5/86	573.500	11/28/86	547.500	26.000	410.900
1988	11/5/87	643.000	11/12/87	678.300	−35.300	375.600
1989	11/7/88	668.200	11/28/88	627.100	41.100	416.700
1990	11/6/89	538.600	11/15/89	566.600	−28.000	388.700
1991	11/5/90	431.800	11/27/90	419.000	12.800	401.500
1992	11/5/91	412.300	11/27/91	412.000	0.300	401.800
1993	11/5/92	397.400	11/27/92	375.700	21.700	423.500
1994	11/5/93	455.100	11/29/93	449.000	6.100	429.600
1995	11/7/94	529.000	11/28/94	519.000	10.000	439.600
1996	11/6/95	534.700	11/27/95	527.700	7.000	446.600
1997	11/5/96	485.900	11/27/96	478.500	7.400	454.000

Trades: 25	Average Profit: 28.85
Winners: 20	Average Loss: −24.60
Losers: 5	% Average Profit: 4.25
% Winners: 80.00	% Average Loss: −3.21

Note: There is a risk of loss in futures trading.

TABLE 8-3 Key Date Seasonal Trade in Short April Platinum (Enter: 12/5; Exit: 12/17; Stop: 7; P/L Ratio: 3.37)

Year	Date In	Price In	Date Out	Price Out	Profit/Loss	Total
1973	12/5/72	145.900	12/18/72	140.000	5.900	5.900
1974	12/5/73	164.500	12/17/73	163.500	1.000	6.900
1975	12/5/74	183.000	12/17/74	176.500	6.500	13.400
1976	12/5/75	146.900	12/17/75	145.700	1.200	14.600
1977	12/6/76	159.200	12/17/76	153.700	5.500	20.100
1978	12/5/77	180.000	12/19/77	179.300	0.700	20.800
1979	12/5/78	326.400	12/18/78	349.000	−22.600	−1.800
1980	12/5/79	552.400	12/17/79	583.400	−31.000	−32.800
1981	12/5/80	659.300	12/17/80	595.500	63.800	31.000
1982	12/7/81	428.000	12/17/81	412.400	15.600	46.600
1983	12/6/82	381.400	12/17/82	366.500	14.900	61.500
1984	12/5/83	414.000	12/19/83	395.700	18.300	79.800
1985	12/5/84	326.500	12/17/84	300.900	25.600	105.400
1986	12/5/85	346.600	12/17/85	336.600	10.000	115.400
1987	12/5/86	484.800	12/17/86	482.100	2.700	118.100
1988	12/7/87	499.500	12/17/87	505.800	−6.300	111.800
1989	12/5/88	600.100	12/19/88	518.800	81.300	193.100
1990	12/5/89	509.300	12/18/89	515.500	−6.200	186.900
1991	12/5/90	429.800	12/17/90	416.400	13.400	200.300
1992	12/5/91	371.800	12/17/91	350.400	21.400	221.700
1993	12/7/92	369.400	12/17/92	363.700	5.700	227.400
1994	12/6/93	379.500	12/17/93	390.100	−10.600	216.800
1995	12/5/94	405.200	12/19/94	418.100	−12.900	203.900
1996	12/5/95	416.200	12/18/95	411.900	4.300	208.200
1997	12/5/96	377.500	12/17/96	373.600	3.900	212.100

Trades: 25 Average Profit: 15.88
Winners: 19 Average Loss: −14.93
Losers: 6 % Average Profit: 3.78
% Winners: 76.00 % Average Loss: −3.50

Note: There is a risk of loss in futures trading.

**TABLE 8-4 Key Date Seasonal Trade in Short October Cotton
(Enter: 7/25; Exit: 8/8; Stop: 7; P/L Ratio: 3.32)**

Year	Date In	Price In	Date Out	Price Out	Profit/Loss	Total
1973	7/25/73	64.500	8/8/73	68.250	−3.750	−3.750
1974	7/25/74	58.200	8/8/74	53.250	4.950	1.200
1975	7/25/75	49.670	8/8/75	49.500	0.170	1.370
1976	7/26/76	78.500	8/9/76	74.270	4.230	5.600
1977	7/25/77	57.130	8/8/77	54.750	2.380	7.980
1978	7/25/78	59.450	8/8/78	61.310	−1.860	6.120
1979	7/25/79	64.620	8/8/79	63.670	0.950	7.070
1980	7/25/80	81.160	7/30/80	87.500	−6.340	0.730
1981	7/27/81	76.470	8/10/81	70.730	5.740	6.470
1982	7/26/82	69.210	8/9/82	66.800	2.410	8.880
1983	7/25/83	79.920	8/8/83	80.000	−0.080	8.800
1984	7/25/84	66.790	8/8/84	66.740	0.050	8.850
1985	7/25/85	60.720	8/8/85	59.170	1.550	10.400
1986	7/25/86	31.880	8/8/86	31.170	0.710	11.110
1987	7/27/87	77.100	8/10/87	76.000	1.100	12.210
1988	7/25/88	58.380	8/8/88	54.470	3.910	16.120
1989	7/25/89	74.400	8/8/89	74.800	−0.400	15.720
1990	7/25/90	77.380	8/8/90	76.580	0.800	16.520
1991	7/25/91	69.080	8/8/91	68.770	0.310	16.830
1992	7/27/92	62.070	8/10/92	61.860	0.210	17.040
1993	7/26/93	60.170	8/9/93	56.230	3.940	20.980
1994	7/25/94	74.150	8/8/94	70.850	3.300	24.280
1995	7/25/95	76.630	8/8/95	73.750	2.880	27.160
1996	7/25/96	71.970	8/8/96	70.300	1.670	28.830

Trades: 24   Average Profit: 2.17
Winners: 19   Average Loss: −2.49
Losers: 5   % Average Profit: 3.30
% Winners: 79.17   % Average Loss: −3.48

Note: There is a risk of loss in futures trading.

**TABLE 8-5 Key Date Seasonal Trade in Short May Heating Oil
(Enter: 2/7; Exit: 2/15; Stop: 5; P/L Ratio: 5.06)**

Year	Date In	Price In	Date Out	Price Out	Profit/Loss	Total
1980	2/7/80	81.350	2/15/80	77.650	3.700	3.700
1981	2/9/81	102.720	2/17/81	99.200	3.520	7.220
1982	2/8/82	80.800	2/16/82	80.550	0.250	7.470
1983	2/7/83	74.340	2/15/83	71.890	2.450	9.920
1984	2/7/84	75.600	2/15/84	74.570	1.030	10.950
1985	2/7/85	69.100	2/15/85	69.860	−0.760	10.190
1986	2/7/86	49.450	2/18/86	45.140	4.310	14.500
1987	2/9/87	48.510	2/17/87	47.230	1.280	15.780
1988	2/8/88	46.650	2/16/88	44.680	1.970	17.750
1989	2/7/89	45.320	2/15/89	45.740	−0.420	17.330
1990	2/7/90	53.910	2/15/90	56.840	−2.930	14.400
1991	2/7/91	53.660	2/15/91	52.130	1.530	15.930
1992	2/7/92	54.700	2/18/92	51.030	3.670	19.600
1993	2/8/93	55.710	2/16/93	54.080	1.630	21.230
1994	2/7/94	45.090	2/15/94	43.410	1.680	22.910
1995	2/7/95	48.500	2/15/95	47.120	1.380	24.290
1996	2/7/96	47.450	2/15/96	49.160	−1.710	22.580
1997	2/7/97	57.720	2/18/97	56.680	1.040	23.620

Trades: 18	Average Profit: 2.10
Winners: 14	Average Loss: −1.46
Losers: 4	% Average Profit: 3.53
% Winners: 77.78	% Average Loss: −2.77

Note: There is a risk of loss in futures trading.

**TABLE 8-6   Key Date Seasonal Trade in Long March Soybeans
(Enter: 10/28; Exit: 11/5; Stop: 8; P/L Ratio: 3.84)**

Year	Date In	Price In	Date Out	Price Out	Profit/Loss	Total
1969	10/28/68	259.250	11/6/68	260.250	1.000	1.000
1970	10/28/69	253.000	11/5/69	254.250	1.250	2.250
1971	10/28/70	315.000	11/5/70	314.375	−0.625	1.625
1972	10/28/71	328.000	11/5/71	329.500	1.500	3.125
1973	10/30/72	363.000	11/6/72	354.750	−8.250	−5.125
1974	10/29/73	542.000	11/5/73	532.500	−9.500	−14.625
1975	10/28/74	788.000	11/6/74	873.250	85.250	70.625
1976	10/28/75	508.250	11/5/75	514.750	6.500	77.125
1977	10/28/76	675.500	11/5/76	677.750	2.250	79.375
1978	10/28/77	550.500	11/7/77	609.250	58.750	138.125
1979	10/30/78	742.250	11/6/78	713.250	−29.000	109.125
1980	10/29/79	685.250	11/5/79	688.750	3.500	112.625
1981	10/28/80	967.250	11/5/80	982.000	14.750	127.375
1982	10/28/81	685.250	11/5/81	694.000	8.750	136.125
1983	10/28/82	563.750	11/5/82	591.000	27.250	163.375
1984	10/28/83	859.500	11/7/83	894.500	35.000	198.375
1985	10/29/84	638.750	11/5/84	645.250	6.500	204.875
1986	10/28/85	525.500	11/5/85	544.250	18.750	223.625
1987	10/28/86	504.000	11/5/86	506.250	2.250	225.875
1988	10/28/87	549.500	11/5/87	552.250	2.750	228.625
1989	10/28/88	797.500	11/7/88	810.500	13.000	241.625
1990	10/30/89	586.500	11/6/89	590.500	4.000	245.625
1991	10/29/90	621.500	11/5/90	612.000	−9.500	236.125
1992	10/28/91	569.750	11/5/91	577.000	7.250	243.375
1993	10/28/92	552.250	11/5/92	550.250	−2.000	241.375
1994	10/28/93	632.750	11/5/93	657.250	24.500	265.875
1995	10/28/94	568.750	11/7/94	575.750	7.000	272.875
1996	10/30/95	686.250	11/6/95	699.500	13.250	286.125
1997	10/28/96	708.500	11/5/96	677.500	−31.000	255.125

Trades: 29	Average Profit: 15.68
Winners: 22	Average Loss: −12.84
Losers: 7	% Average Profit: 2.40
% Winners: 75.86	% Average Loss: −2.06

Note: There is a risk of loss in futures trading.

is no guarantee that the same key date seasonal trade will indeed be profitable in future years. The key date seasonal tendency is merely that: a tendency. Measures must be taken to avoid the probability of large losses. Losses must be limited according to the specifications of the original key date calculation.

GENERAL RULES

The following general rules apply to key date seasonal trades as I have researched them:

1. *Trade is entered on the close of the ideal entry date.* If the ideal entry date is a weekend or a market holiday, then entry is on the close of the next business day.

2. *Trade is held with indicated stop loss.* Stop loss is the closing basis. In other words, the market must close below the stop loss if in a long position or above the stop loss if in a short position.

3. *The position is exited, with profit or loss, on the ideal exit date on the close.* If the market is closed on the ideal exit date, then trade is closed out at the end of the next business day.

There are many variations on the theme of key date seasonals. I am researching hundreds of such trades, and anyone else with access to a computer and sufficient historical data can do the same. In addition to the raw dates themselves, various money management techniques, methods of adding to positions, and methods of using trailing stops could considerably improve or optimize the results of seasonal key date trades.

I have listed 11 key date seasonals along with their statistics in Appendix D.

9

AN OVERVIEW OF SEASONAL TRADING SYSTEMS, METHODS, AND CONCEPTS

The preceding chapters have explained seasonality in its various forms and theories as they apply to futures trading. There is much to understand and still more to put into practice. It may, in fact, seem to you that there are too many choices. Perhaps this overview will help put matters into perspective.

METHODS OF APPLICATION OF CASH SEASONALITY

As you know from reading Chapter 3, the recommended use of monthly cash seasonals is in longer time frames—from 1 month to as long as 12 months. The reality of futures trading is that only rarely does an individual hold a futures position for more than several months (unless, of course, the position is a loser). The simple fact of futures life is that traders tend to exit their winning trades quickly while they keep their losing trades for a long time in the hope—indeed, the dream—that the losses will be reversed. In practice, losing trades tend to remain losers unless things change quickly after initial trade entry. It is therefore

119

unrealistic to expect that too many traders will use the monthly cash seasonal trends and tendencies for establishing and holding positions that they intend to keep for major seasonal moves.

As an example, consider the fact that wheat prices tend to bottom in the June to July time frame, trending higher through year-end. In order to take advantage of this well-established seasonal tendency, the trader would need to be prepared to buy in June or July and to hold until late in the year or possibly early in the next year. During the span of up to eight months that the trade would need to be held, the odds are quite high that the trader will lose patience, be stopped out, or abandon the position as soon as a small profit has been made. Iron discipline is needed in order for large and lengthy moves to be followed. For those relatively few individuals who can follow the seasonal rules, the use of monthly cash seasonals is highly recommended.

USING CASH SEASONALS

Typically people who trade for large moves over time frames of up to 11 months are commercial traders, grain firms, savvy farmers, and highly disciplined, systematic traders. This is a rare breed, limited to very few traders. But for those who can follow the secular seasonal moves, the rewards can be considerable. How can these large moves be captured? I have several suggestions.

Cash Monthly Seasonal Trend Compared to Actual Trend

One way to participate in larger seasonal moves is to compare the current market trend with the average seasonal trend. To accomplish this, examine the current weekly or monthly price trend in the futures contract you wish to trade. Then compare the trend to the monthly cash seasonal composite trend for the given market. If the two are essentially similar, it is reasonable to expect that the market is on its typical seasonal trend and that the trend should continue. It is therefore reasonable to establish a position consistent with the seasonal trend expectation(s). The position could be a flat position, a spread position consistent with the market trend, an options position consistent with the market trend, or an options spread consistent with the existing market trend. In all cases risk management must also be a necessary component of the approach. Either a dead stop (a prede-termined dollar risk amount) or a percentage stop loss of entry price will be sufficient to manage risk. Although the use of a risk-managing stop loss will likely decrease overall accuracy, it will also significantly decrease drawdown.

Cash Monthly Seasonal Trend and Timing

A more "refined" way to take advantage of well-established seasonal trends is to use the monthly cash seasonals with timing. This is also a relatively simple procedure. To accomplish this goal, you will need to use one or two of the many market-timing indicators that are available today: moving averages, moving average convergence divergence, sto-chastics, the relative strength index, directional movement indicator, momentum, rate of change, parabolic, on-balance volume, various os-cillators, accumulation/distribution, or any of a host of other timing signals, each with its good and bad points. (Even astrology should work if it says to go long during the time frame of a usually bullish cash sea-sonal trend.) Be sure that if you apply any of the cash seasonal meth-ods described here, you focus on those months showing relatively high-probability moves in the same direction. Simply look at the arrows on the charts in Appendix A.

There are many timing indicators to use; in fact, there are literally hundreds. It is very likely that as long as timing and seasonal trend are both pointing in the same direction, the seasonal will be more likely to occur. Consider the following possibilities in using ideal seasonal trend and timing:

• *Ideal seasonal is bullish but timing is bearish.* Do not follow the seasonal trend until timing turns bullish within the ideal seasonal up-trend. This could occur prior to the bottom of the seasonal trend, at about the same time as the bottom, or after the ideal seasonal trend has turned bullish. The time window here is relatively broad. As a rule of thumb, timing can turn bullish up to several months prior to the ideal seasonal upturn. A simple way to deal with such a situation is to buy as soon as the ideal seasonal is bullish as long as the timing indi-cator(s) are bullish at the same time.

• *Ideal seasonal is bearish but timing is bullish.* Do not follow the seasonal trend until timing turns bearish within the ideal seasonal downtrend. This could occur prior to the bottom of the seasonal trend, at about the same time as the top, or after the ideal seasonal trend has turned bearish. The time window here is relatively broad. As a rule of thumb, timing can turn bearish up to several months prior to the ideal seasonal downturn. A simple way to deal with such a situation is to sell short as soon as the ideal seasonal is bearish, as long as your timing indicator(s) are bearish at the same time.

• *Ideal seasonal is bullish and timing is bullish.* The decision here is simple. As long as both indicators point in the same direction at the same time, you can buy. Naturally, there is no guarantee that profits will result; however, the odds of success are likely to be higher inasmuch as both indicators agree.

• *Ideal seasonal is bearish and timing is bearish.* The decision here is simple. As long as both indicators point in the bearish direction at the same time, you can sell. Naturally, there is no guarantee that profits will result; however, the odds of success are likely to be higher inasmuch as both indicators agree.

I suggest using two timing indicators that are not based on the same data or theory—for example, a momentum-based indicator with an oscillator, a moving average–based indicator with a contrary opinion indicator, or a contrary opinion indicator with a volume/open interest–based indicator. When all three are in agreement, your likelihood of success should be higher than merely following the seasonal without timing. Of course, you will miss some moves, and you will trade less under such conditions, but trading less frequently is not necessarily a bad thing.

Monthly Cash Seasonal and Contrary Opinion Indicators

There are a number of contrary opinion indicators currently used by traders, based on the theory that the majority of traders are often wrong at significant market turning points. The most popular contrary opinion data are provided by Market Vane (Pasadena, California) and the Daily Sentiment Index (available from my office in Northbrook, Illinois). In addition, the United States Department of Agriculture releases its Commitment of Traders Report (COT) regularly. These reports provide information about the breakdown of long versus short positions held by the trading public (small traders) and professionals (large traders). Although the COT is a useful report, it is often out of date by the time it is released. Market Vane provides weekly as well as daily sentiment data, and I provide daily sentiment data through my Daily Sentiment Index (DSI).

In order to use sentiment in conjunction with the ideal monthly seasonal trend, watch for sentiment to become very low (the majority of traders is bearish) at seasonal lows and to become very high (the majority of traders is bullish) at seasonal highs. There are many modifications and ramifications of this approach. You could also use a hybrid method that combines timing, market sentiment, and seasonality.

Monthly Seasonal Cash Trend and Support and Resistance

Still another method of using monthly cash seasonals is what I have termed the *seasonal trend support/resistance* method. The first step is to determine if the current trend is consistent with the ideal or average seasonal trend. If they are consistent, you will trade *only* in the direction of the trend using a support/resistance method as your technique for buying or selling.

Consider the following possibilities:

• *The seasonal trend is bullish.* In this case, you will be a buyer at technical support levels. There are various methods of computing technical support levels. Among these are support trend lines, channel support, percentage retracements, my moving average channel (MAC) support, and a variety of other methods, including such esoteric techniques as Gann angles, Elliott waves, and Fibonacci numbers. I cannot attest to the validity of these methods other than my MAC, which I find to be very useful in determining trend, support, and resistance.

The MAC is a simple approach that consists of a 10-period moving average of highs and an 8-period moving average of lows. When two consecutive price bars are entirely above the 10-period moving average of highs, an uptrend is triggered. When this occurs, support is defined as the 8-period moving average of the lows. When two consecutive price bars are entirely below the 8-day moving average of the lows, a downtrend is triggered. In this case, the 10-day moving average of highs is defined as resistance.

If the seasonal trend is bullish, then you will be a buyer at the 8-day moving average of lows. You will not be a seller inasmuch as the seasonal trend is bullish. The only selling you will do is to exit long positions.

• *The seasonal trend is bearish.* If the seasonal trend is bearish and the current trend is consistent with the seasonal, then you will be a seller at resistance but not a buyer. Your only buying will be for the purpose of covering short positions. You may use the MAC trend change signals to determine if the current trend is consistent with the seasonal trend. You may use other techniques for determining the trend, as well as support and resistance if you wish, as long as you follow the general guidelines above.

• *Timing fails to confirm a seasonal trend.* In this case you will take no action until or unless the trend determination method you are using is consistent with the anticipated seasonal tendency.

Weekly Seasonal Futures Tendencies

There are several ways in which to use the weekly seasonal futures tendencies, already described in Chapter 4. In essence, the methods of application are no different from those described above for monthly seasonal cash tendencies. The only difference is that you will be dealing with weekly patterns rather than monthly patterns. You may also use the MAC method.

Daily Seasonal Futures Tendencies

There are several ways in which to use the daily seasonal futures tendencies, described in Chapter 6. The methods of application are no different from those described in the monthly seasonal cash tendencies; however, the time frame of application will be different. Signals of trend change as well as support and resistance levels in this case are gathered from hourly data, or even 30-minute data, since the time frame is considerably shorter.

Key Date Seasonal Trades

Key data seasonal trades (KDTs) are specific to date and time of day for entry and exit; hence, they are a stand-alone method. Some traders may wish to use timing with KDTs, an acceptable practice. Theoretically the use of timing to confirm trend and anticipated KDT should improve the odds of success. Hence, if the KDT signals a buy on a given date and if a short-term timing indicator (hourly or 30 minute, perhaps even daily) is bullish, then the KDT odds of success should improve.

Seasonal Spreads and Timing

The use of timing indicators with daily, weekly, and KDT seasonal spreads is similar to what has been described above. The use of timing indicators for spread trades should increase their accuracy. There are a number of timing methods that may be used with spreads, including traditional support, resistance, and breakout points, as well as my recommended rate of change/moving average method. This approach consists of using a 24- to 28-day moving average or the 24- to 28-day rate of change for the given spread. See Figures 9-1 through 9.9.

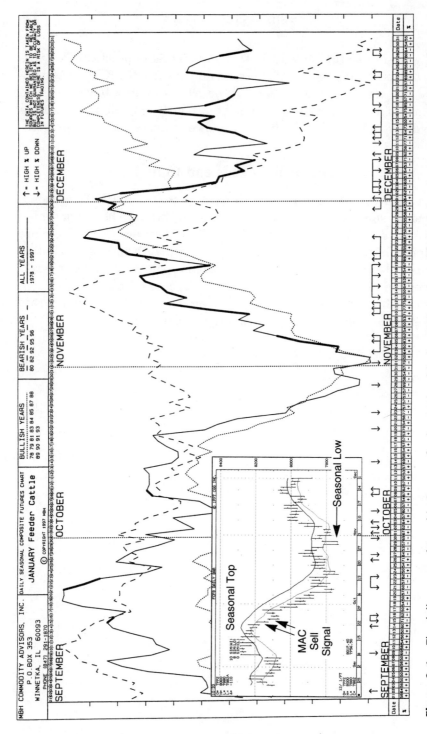

Figure 9-1 The daily seasonal trend in January feeder cattle with the 1998 contract and MAC signals. (Composite chart copyright © 1997 by MBH Commodity Advisors, Inc.; inset chart reprinted with permission of CQG, Inc.)

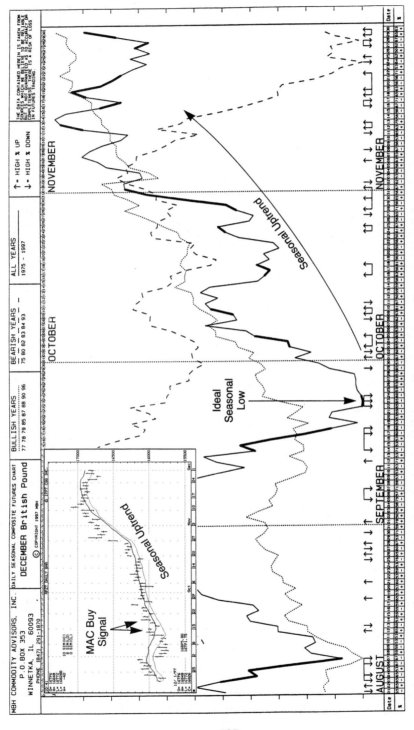

Figure 9-2 The daily seasonal trend in December British pound futures and December 1997 British pound futures with timing. (Composite chart copyright © 1997 by MBH Commodity Advisors, Inc.; inset chart reprinted with permission of CQG, Inc.)

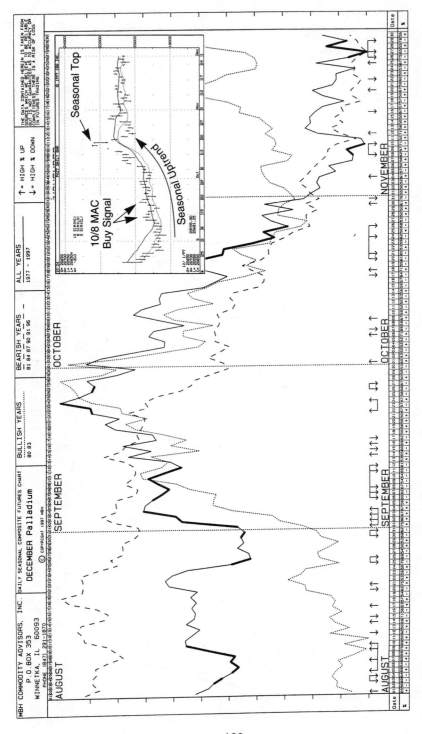

Figure 9-3 The daily seasonal pattern in December palladium futures compared to the actual 1997 trend and signals. (Composite chart copyright © 1997 by MBH Commodity Advisors, Inc.; inset chart reprinted with permission of CQG, Inc.)

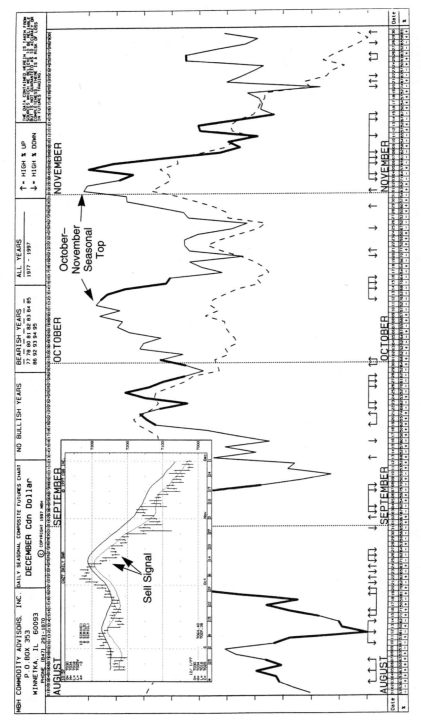

Figure 9-4 The daily seasonal tendency in December Canadian dollars with actual 1997 December trend and timing. (Composite chart copyright © 1997 by MBH Commodity Advisors, Inc.; inset chart reprinted with permission of CQG, Inc.)

129

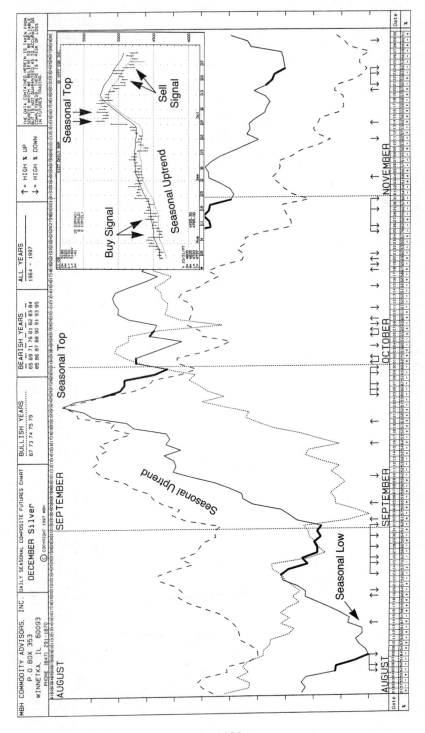

Figure 9-5 December silver futures daily seasonal tendency with 1997 December trend and timing. (Composite chart copyright © 1997 by MBH Commodity Advisors, Inc.; inset chart reprinted with permission of CQG, Inc.)

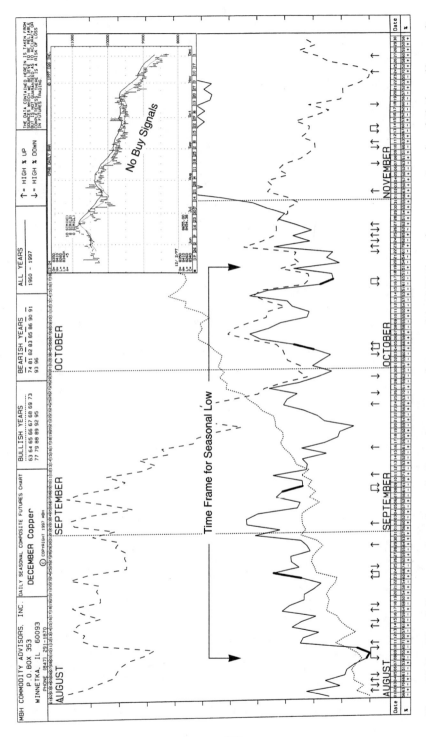

Figure 9-6 The daily seasonal tendency in December copper futures with 1997 December copper trend and timing. (Composite chart copyright © 1997 by MBH Commodity Advisors, Inc.; inset chart reprinted with permission of CQG, Inc.)

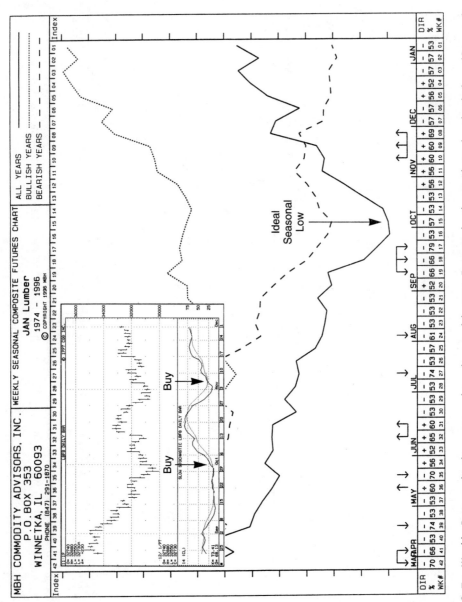

Figure 9-7 Weekly January lumber seasonal tendency with 1998 January lumber and stochastic timing. (Composite chart copyright © 1996 by MBH Commodity Advisors, Inc.; inset chart reprinted with permission of CQG, Inc.)

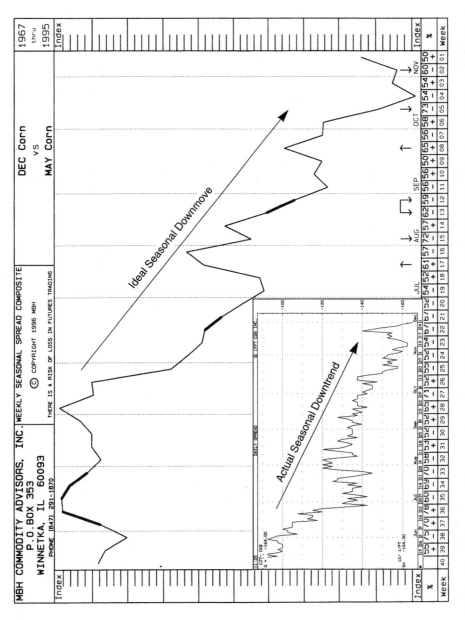

Figure 9-8 December versus May corn spread, weekly seasonal trend and 1997–1998 actual spread. (Composite chart copyright © 1996 by MBH Commodity Advisors, Inc.; inset chart reprinted with permission of CQG, Inc.)

133

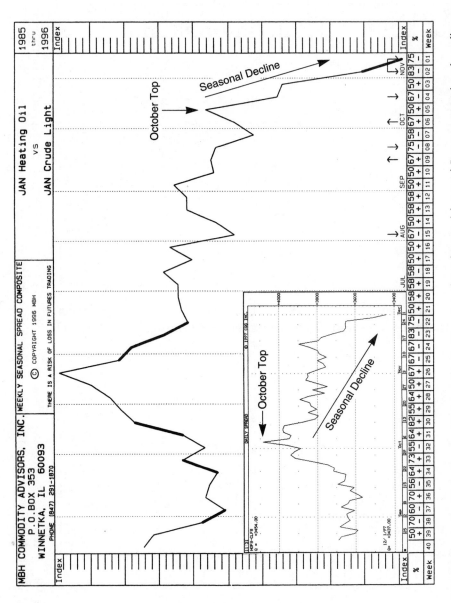

Figure 9-9 January heating oil versus January crude oil seasonal tendency with actual January 1998 heating oil versus 1998 January crude oil spread. (Composite chart copyright © 1996 by MBH Commodity Advisors, Inc.; inset chart reprinted with permission of CQG, Inc.)

134

10

COMBINING SEASONALITY WITH TIMING

Although there are many ways in which seasonal price patterns may be used without confirming the existing trend of a market, some traders feel that filtering seasonals by using technical timing indicators yields better results. I know of no study that definitively validates this assertion; however, it does appear that such a method has face validity. Logically, it seems reasonable that markets currently in uptrends would be more likely to make seasonal rallies than would markets in downtrends, and vice versa for bearish seasonals. I cannot present any definitive evidence in support of this belief, but it does seem reasonable and logical. For those who wish to combine the two, I offer the following suggestions and illustrations.

TIMING INDICATORS

There are literally hundreds, and perhaps thousands, of timing indicators. Any trader with a computer and data history can conjure up a new timing indicator at least once daily. The bottom line of most timing indicators is that they are typically effective about 50 percent of the time *unless* they are confirmed by another timing indicator that is *not* derived from the same type of calculation or data. Dyed-in-the-wool technicians would disagree with me, but I would stick to my case: most timing indicators, when used with risk management rules, regress to the mean. Only a precious few are reliable slightly more than chance. However, I have found that combining two indicators that are determined on the basis of different data or using different mathematical models is more likely to be effective when they both yield the same result at about the same time. Hence, when a moving average–based indicator, for example, correlates with a market sentiment–based indicator, the odds are higher that they will be successful than if either was used alone.

Hence, if we consider seasonals to be timing indicators in a general sense, then virtually any indicator that is not seasonally based would be reasonable to use in conjunction with seasonals.

Here are the timing indicators that I have found useful in my work with seasonals:

- *Double and triple moving average crossovers.* These indicators (and there are many of them) are lagging indicators. As a result, they tend to give enter signals after the trend of a market has changed. If the length of the moving averages is too large, then the delay in entry could be costly, since the seasonal tendency may have ended or may be close to ending when the signal is triggered. It is therefore very important to set the correct lengths for the moving averages if this situation is to be avoided. Note also that market exit using moving averages is often delayed and could occur well after a trend has changed. This could erase profits and turn them into losses if the length of the moving averages is not correct.

- *Stochastics and relative strength indicator.* Both of these are essentially the same. They are less likely to give false signals than are traditional moving average–based methods. As in the case of moving averages, it is important to set the indicator length correctly in order to avoid false signals and late signals. As a rule of thumb (and this is a very general rule), I advise setting the indicator length at about 25 percent the length of the seasonal trade. Assume, for example, that a key date seasonal trade runs 45 days in length. You would use a stochastic or relative strength index (RSI) length of about 25 percent of the 45 days. This would work to about 11 days. For trade lengths over 75 days, I recommend using a 28-day stochastic or a 14-day RSI. These values are not written in stone; you can and should experiment with them.

- *Daily market sentiment.* The daily sentiment index (DSI) is calculated daily. It is a non-price-based indicator that merely measures the percentage of traders who are bullish on each of 31 U.S. markets at the end of each trading day. Since the DSI is a contrary opinion indicator, a very low DSI (10 percent or less) during the ideal time frame of a seasonal low would be taken as bullish confirmation of the low, whereas a very high DSI (90 percent or more) during the time frame of a seasonal top suggests a higher probability that the top will occur.

- *Momentum (rate of change).* This is a good timing indicator when used with its own moving average as a crossover method. This simple but powerful approach appears to have particularly good reliability when used with seasonal spreads.

- *Moving average channel.* The moving average channel (MAC) method is a technique I developed for marketing timing in all time frames. It is described more fully in my books *Short-Term Trading in Futures* (Winnetka, Ill.: MBH Inc., 1994) and *The Compleat Day-Trader* (New York: McGraw-Hill, 1995).

- *Parabolic.* The parabolic method of timing can also be used effectively when entering seasonal positions. Consult a good book on technical analysis for a description of the parabolic method and its construction.[1]

- *Moving average convergence divergence indicator.* Developed by Jerry Appel,[2] this indicator can be used in conjunction with seasonal patterns. You will need to use some judgment in deter-

---

[1]Titles include *How the Futures Market Works* by Jacob Bernstein (New York: New York Institute of Finance, 1990); *The New Commodity Trading Systems and Methods* by Perry Kaufman (New York: Wiley, 1987); and *New Concepts in Technical Trading Systems* by J. Welles Wilder, Jr. (Greensboro, N.C.: Trend Research, 1978).

[2]Gerald Appel, *Winning Market Systems* (Great Neck, N.Y.: Signalert, 1974).

mining the length of your timing indicators. This aspect is crucial
to the effective use of market timing with seasonal patterns.

EXAMPLES OF TIMING AND SEASONALITY

Following is a selection of examples and illustrations in various time
frames with a variety of seasonal patterns in a number of different
markets. The best way to illustrate these applications is by examining
the charts and their corresponding commentary. In so doing you will
gain a good grasp of how to combine the two elements. There is a certain degree of art to this procedure; there are no hard-and-fast, purely
operational, and totally objective rules of application. Nevertheless,
with some study and analysis, you can develop a set of entry and exit
parameters into a systematic approach. Note that I consider key
date seasonal trading to be a completely objective and mechanical approach. One could easily build in a "trade" or "do not trade" confirming
indicator with key date trades. Key date seasonals lend themselves
more readily to such an application than do the seasonal futures and
cash charts.

September Coffee and Moving Average Channel Timing

Figure 10-1 shows the weekly seasonal composite chart for September
coffee futures, with the inset at the bottom left the daily December
1997 coffee futures chart. The seasonal chart shows that a top is often
made in early May. The actual chart for 1997 shows that the trend re-
mained bullish until early June. The moving average channel (MAC)
indicator did not give a sell signal. In early June, however, it gave a
daily sell signal. This occurred within the time frame of an ideal seasonal decline on the weekly composite seasonal chart. The MAC signal
also occurred during a period of down arrows (which indicate higher
probability of decline). Hence, the seasonal and the timing indicators
worked well together.

Note that a seasonal low point was due in August. At this time, the
MAC indicator would be used to exit the short position and reverse to
a long position. Traders wishing to fine-tune entry could move to a
short-term time frame (even hourly data) in order to generate signals.

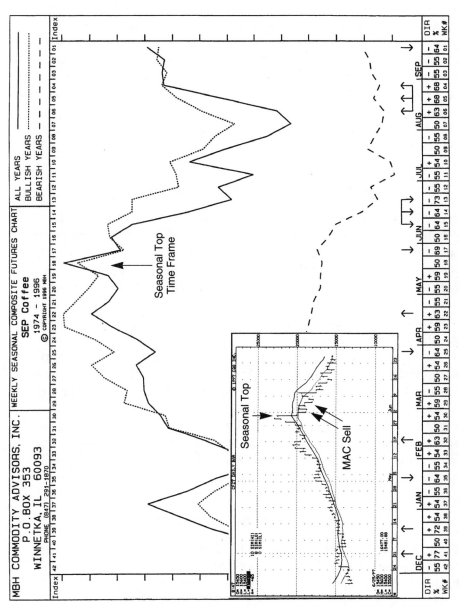

Figure 10-1 Weekly seasonal composite chart for September coffee futures, with daily December 1997 coffee futures chart. (Composite chart copyright © 1996 by MBH Commodity Advisors, Inc.; inset chart reprinted with permission of CQG, Inc.)

139

December Cocoa and Stochastic Timing

Figure 10-2 shows the weekly seasonal composite chart for December cocoa futures. The chart shows an ideal seasonal low in April, and I have marked the ideal low time accordingly. I have also included a daily futures chart for December 1997 cocoa futures (see the figure). The daily chart shows a 28-day slow stochastic indicator used for timing. I have marked the stochastic "buy signal" accordingly. Subsequent to the stochastic buy signal, prices moved higher, very much in line with their ideal seasonal uptrend. Here is another case in which timing and seasonals were compatible.

September Palladium and MAC Timing

Figure 10-3 shows the daily seasonal composite chart for September palladium futures. Although the palladium market is thinly traded (it has a low trading volume), as a market, it has shown some fairly reliable seasonal characteristics. The daily seasonal futures chart shows that the period from late May through early June has typically reached seasonal lows.

I have included a daily chart of the actual prices for December 1997 palladium (Figure 10-3, inset) plotted against my MAC timing indicator. As you can see, an MAC buy signal was generated in mid-April, well ahead of ideal seasonal low. In this situation, the trader would wait until the daily seasonal composite trend was up before entering. Therefore, in mid-May, when the MAC indicator was still bullish, a long position could have been taken since both indicators were in agreement. The uptrend was anticipated based on the daily seasonal composite chart. The combination of seasonals and timing was effective in this case.

December Heating Oil and MAC Timing

Now look at Figure 10-4. It shows the ideal time frame for a seasonal low in heating oil futures as being in early July. The inset chart shows the December 1997 heating oil futures daily chart plotted with the MAC timing indicator. As of the end of the daily 1997 chart, there had been no timing work to indicate a bottom. Hence, the trader using timing and seasonality would still be waiting for a signal to enter.

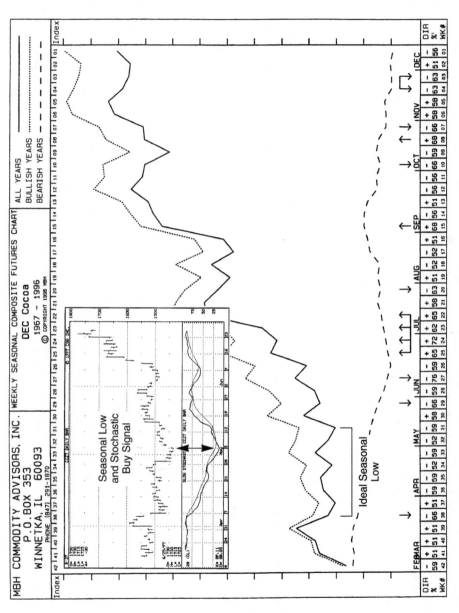

Figure 10-2 Weekly seasonal composite chart for December cocoa futures, with daily December 1997 cocoa futures chart. (Composite chart copyright © 1996 by MBH Commodity Advisors, Inc.; inset chart reprinted with permission of CQG, Inc.)

141

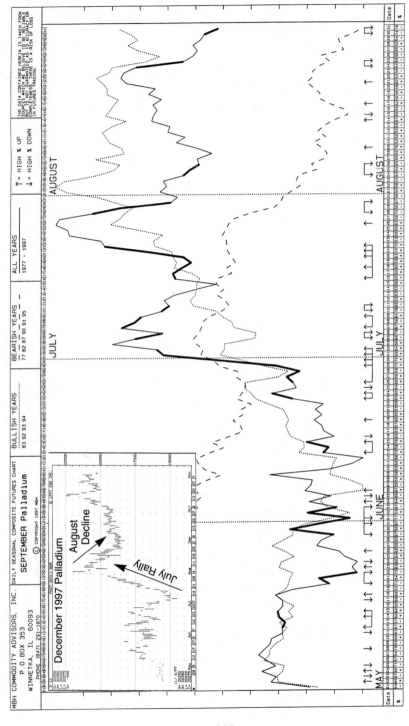

Figure 10-3 Daily seasonal composite chart for September palladium futures, with daily December 1997 palladium futures chart. (Composite chart copyright © 1997 by MBH Commodity Advisors, Inc.; inset chart reprinted with permission of CQG, Inc.)

142

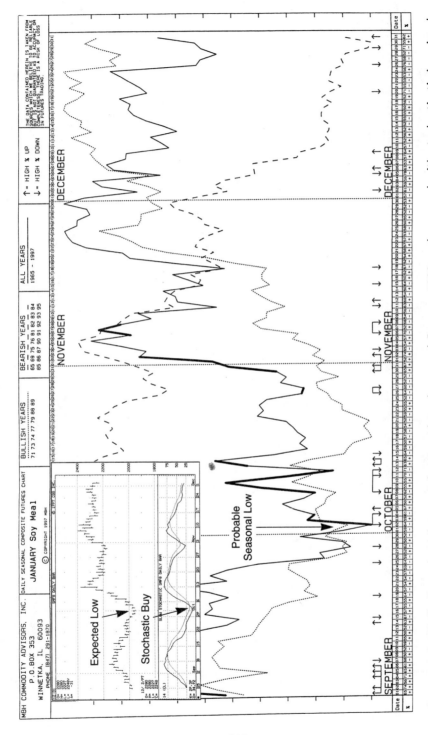

Figure 10-4 Daily January soybean meal seasonal tendency and January 1998 soybean meal with stochastic timing signal. (Composite chart copyright © 1997 by MBH Commodity Advisors, Inc.; inset chart reprinted with permission of CQG, Inc.)

143

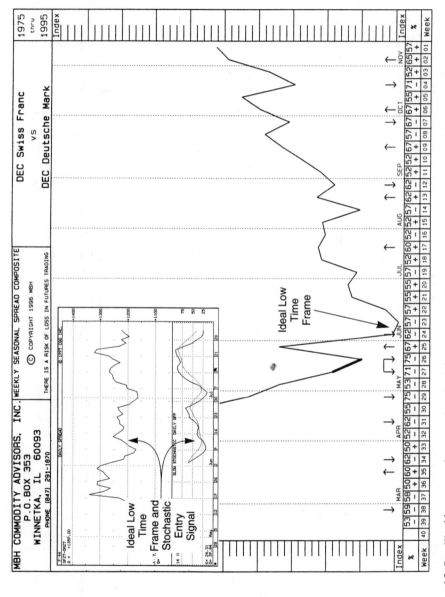

Figure 10-5 Weekly seasonal composite chart for December Swiss franc versus December deutsche mark futures spread, with 60-minute December 1997 Swiss franc versus December deutsche mark futures chart. (Composite chart copyright © 1996 by MBH Commodity Advisors, Inc.; inset chart reprinted with permission of CQG, Inc.)

144

Swiss Franc Versus Deutsche Mark Spread and Stochastics

Figure 10-5 shows the weekly seasonal composite spread chart for December Swiss franc versus December deutsche mark spread. This is a popular spread, which, based on the chart, has shown a tendency to gain in favor of the Swiss franc from early June through November. The accompanying 60-minute chart shows how the 28-day stochastic indicator turned bullish in the right time frame, indicating that entry was reasonable.

11

CONCLUSIONS AND SUGGESTIONS FOR FURTHER RESEARCH

This book does not constitute the final word on seasonal analysis. Very few, if any, market analysts have all of the answers. In fact, most of us seek only to become proficient at finding some of the answers. It has been repeatedly demonstrated in the marketplace that having access to only several workable keys can frequently lead to the accumulation of large trading profits. The world of commodity futures trading is expanding at such a rapid pace that it is virtually impossible for any individual to have at hand most of the information that affects any given market or group of markets. In realization of this fact, my efforts through the years have been to focus on repetitive patterns. Whether these take the form of price patterns, technical patterns, cyclical patterns, or seasonal patterns has been, and continues to be, of relatively little importance to me. The fact that patterns do occur has been and continues to be of major importance to me. To a certain extent, patterns are very much a function of perception.

Many times the naked eye will fail to detect patterns that are clearly visible and observable but that, for various reasons, cannot be seen. The psychology of gestalt has had much to say about such perceptual anomalies. Often a trader's perception will be affected by internal and external forces that have no direct bearing on the markets themselves but are nevertheless influential in either distorting or clarifying interpretation of market patterns. Such forces include a trader's personality, his or her inner conflicts, and his or her financial obligations. The goal of technical analysis through the years has been to minimize such distortions and misperceptions by imposing a rigid set of criteria on analysts who are making financial judgments based on such interpretations. The computer revolution has further minimized potential errors in the identification and assessment of market patterns.

Paradoxically, iterative processes involving literally billions of test patterns have complicated the job of speculators by providing them with an oversupply of patterns that they must watch in the analytical process. I suspect that there is still considerable research of this nature to perform on seasonal price patterns that should yield a wealth of information on seasonality. Indeed, my own efforts have barely exposed the tip of the iceberg when it comes to seasonal analysis, and yet I have done considerably more seasonal research than have most other analysts. I strongly suggest that the work explained in this book should be used as a starting point for further research rather than a resting point. Futures professionals and traders have a tendency to become complacent in their knowledge of the markets. The markets, however, are ever growing in size, scope, and complexity, and so traders must grow in their understanding of market analyses and research applications.

Now that computer technology is within the reach of virtually every speculator and investor, all efforts should be made to allow computers to do what they do best: number crunching, or the iterative process by which many trial-and-error judgments are made using a given statistical method or procedure, the object of which is to refine the formula or procedure being tested to the point where its results are at their maximum. Such procedures that are easily performed on a computer will add further evidence that seasonality exists and has not undergone appreciable changes in the past 100 years or more. Additionally, it will show that seasonality can be used as either part of a trading system or an adjunct to other trading systems not based primarily on seasonality.

CAVEATS

No book on futures trading would be complete without a clearly worded and specific statement regarding the risk inherent in such trading. It has, of course, been acceptable procedure to state such risks in the form of a standard disclaimer. However, such a statement is far too simple and serves only to warn but not necessarily to teach. To tell someone, "Don't touch the stove," constitutes a warning. To tell someone, "Don't touch the stove; it will burn you," constitutes a warning in addition to a statement of risk. To tell someone, "Don't touch the stove there; it will burn you. However, if you touch it in the right places, you can achieve your intended goal without fear of being burned," not only warns or explains the risks but also teaches alternatives.

The standard futures disclaimer constitutes nothing but a warning. The following list gives you specific warnings as to what may occur, why these things may happen, and, most important, what you can and should do in order to overcome or avoid them:

1. *Don't put too much trust in seasonals.* Don't fall victim to the syndrome of believing too strongly in any one or group of seasonal patterns. No matter how strong the statistical support may be in favor of a given trend, the fact remains that seasonality and history are not perfect. Therefore, any rules that you implement for stop losses and other risk-limiting methods must not be altered or adjusted for what you feel to be a potentially high-probability seasonal trading opportunity. In other words, all seasonal trades are created equal; they must not be tampered with since the potential loss may be larger than acceptable.

2. *Be prepared to lose.* In a world where most futures transactions are closed out at losses, any individual, regardless of trading system, who is not prepared to take a loss is not admitting to reality. The attitude that develops from being unprepared to take a loss is also one that will foster the third evil on my list.

3. *Don't ride a loss.* Traders are often tempted to ride losing positions; not to take a loss is, in some traders' minds, preferable to the admission that a system failed to work and that a bad decision was made. This is also a dangerous undertaking since it inevitably leads in the long run to losses that are larger than they should be. This undermines

the overall profitability of all trading systems. In many cases, it may seem more reasonable to stay with a losing position because of the manner in which seasonal futures tendencies operate. In other words, seasonal tendencies are often given too much credibility by traders who seek to justify holding on to a losing position. Their reasoning may be simply that the seasonal suggests an uptrend for several weeks yet. Although the reliability readings may be poor, traders may take refuge in what is expected, using it to justify riding a loss. This is a bad procedure.

4. *Keep research up to date.* Seasonals change. Some become stronger, some weaker. In order to remain in close touch with changes, I strongly recommend updating seasonal price tendency data every year—at the very minimum, every two years. This work is rather simple to do on your own, provided you have access to a database of reasonably good length.

5. *Avoid extraneous input.* Perhaps the greatest failing of most futures traders is that they complicate their systems and methods with information overload. Some people believe that there is no such thing as too much information in the futures market. They reason that the more information that they have at their disposal, the more likely they will be to succeed. I doubt whether such reasoning is valid, and it may very well be the case that there is an inverse relationship between trader success and information input. Consequently, I advise strict limitation of information sources when using the seasonal price patterns or trading approaches described in this book. The majority of methods I have described are strictly technical in nature and do not require the input of any fundamental information.

6. *Be consistent.* Perhaps one of the greatest errors a person can commit is inconsistency. Inconsistency results in faulty learning and usually fosters the development of ineffective or inappropriate trading habits. People who have acquired that habit will find it difficult to relearn effective habits and will likely lose money in the process.[1] Consistency is a difficult trading habit to acquire, but it is perhaps the most valuable asset a trader can possess.

---

[1]The topic of trading consistency and investor psychology is presented at length in my *The Investor's Quotient—The Psychology of Successful Speculation in Commodities and Stocks* (New York: Wiley, 1980).

7. *Avoid contraseasonal markets.* Markets that have behaved contrary to seasonal expectations early in the year or early in the contract month tend to remain relatively erratic throughout the life of their contract. Therefore, it is usually best to avoid trading in such markets, particularly after the market has established itself as either unpredictable or contraseasonal.

I have shown the existence of seasonal price tendencies in such diverse markets as interest rates, petroleum, lumber, metals, and foreign currencies. It might seem that these markets are not necessarily related and that one might therefore not expect to find any reliable seasonal price tendencies. But a close examination of the markets clearly indicates that most of them are indeed interrelated and, for a variety of reasons, exhibit seasonal variation.

I have perhaps left several potential areas of application unexplored. I leave this task to those creative individuals who can take my seasonal research as the starting point for more study. The application of seasonality as a viable trading strategy has been relatively unexplored for too many years. Further applications research is clearly justified.

CHANGING SEASONALS?

I have often been asked about the possibility of seasonal price patterns' changing over time, perhaps as a function of changing weather patterns or changing perceptions of weather patterns and their effect on speculators. In addition, changes in the ability of producers to alter their growing season by planting various varieties of seeds, using new irrigation techniques, and multiple cropping may also affect seasonal price patterns. The entry of foreign competitors into markets that in the past were primarily dominated by the United States (e.g., Brazil is now producing significant soybean crops) might also affect seasonals. In answer to questions asked about what one might do in response to such situations, I can say only that continuing research is the most logical answer. It is only by applying an ongoing program of research that speculators will be able to detect changes before losing too much money on a previously well-established pattern that is no longer functioning in its usual fashion. (This is true in any field, of course.)

The importance of continuing research, updating statistics, and continuing interpretation of results is necessary to remaining current. It is for this reason that I regularly publish updates of my seasonal futures charts and seasonal cash charts. Given current microcomputer technology, those who have access to reliable cash and futures price data can generate their own seasonal price charts according to the various techniques and indexes described in this book. Those who wish to keep in touch with my updates may contact me at MBH Commodity Advisors, Inc., P.O. Box 353, Winnetka, IL 60093. I stress, however, that the work required to update seasonal price patterns can be easily done on one's own, provided the time commitment can be made.

I end with one note of encouragement and one note of warning. I will dispense with the warning first. You will know from reading this book that I have gone to great lengths to warn you not only about the risks inherent in futures trading but also about the risks inherent in using seasonal price indicators. Those who adhere closely to the rules of seasonality and the trading suggestions I have made throughout this book should fare better than the average futures trader should. However, I have no ultimate control as to the fashion in which individual traders implement these seasonal trading tools and strategies. Any tool may be abused, and the results of such abuse will certainly not be favorable to the individual who is guilty of improper implementation or unrealistic expectations. I caution you one final time to apply seasonal trading strategies, rules, research, and indicators in a logical and consistent fashion using the accepted principles of conservative money management and trading skills. To do otherwise will subvert and circumvent the efficacy of established seasonal price tendencies.

Finally, here is the encouragement. I sincerely believe, after spending many years researching seasonal price tendencies, that futures traders and commercial or agricultural producers who have a working knowledge of seasonal price patterns as well as a close knowledge of specific seasonal tendencies are probably several steps ahead of average speculators. By virtue of this knowledge, traders can apply more specific timing, crop marketing, forward purchasing, and forward sales to the specifics of their needs in the futures market. The benefits that can accrue are considerable, particularly to those who have had experience with the techniques and know when, where, and how to apply them for maximum results.

APPENDIX A

EXAMINING DAILY SEASONAL CASH TENDENCIES

Figures A-1 through A-16 are some selected daily seasonal futures charts. Considerable space is given to presenting these charts because there is no better way to illustrate the important seasonals than visually. Furthermore, no book on seasonal price patterns could claim to be complete without including these charts. They are a source of both reference and information and will remain reasonably current for perhaps several years. However, as time passes, seasonal tendencies change—some becoming stronger, some weaker. Those who regularly use and follow seasonal price patterns in their marketing, hedging, or speculating programs should use up-to-date information. I am certain that you will find yourself turning to these pages repeatedly .

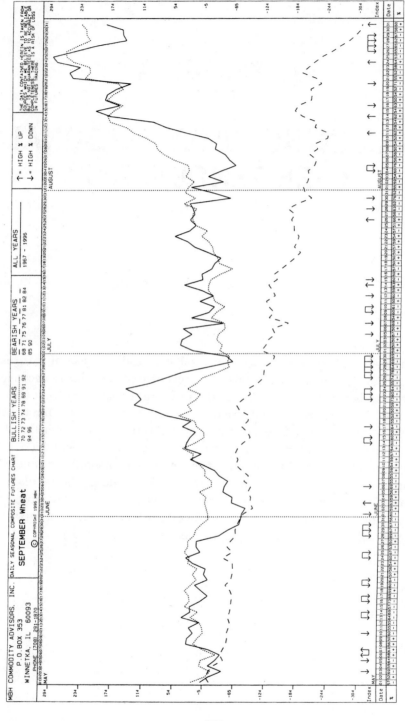

Figure A-1 Daily seasonal futures chart, September wheat, 1967–1996. (Copyright © 1996 by MBH Commodity Advisors, Inc.)

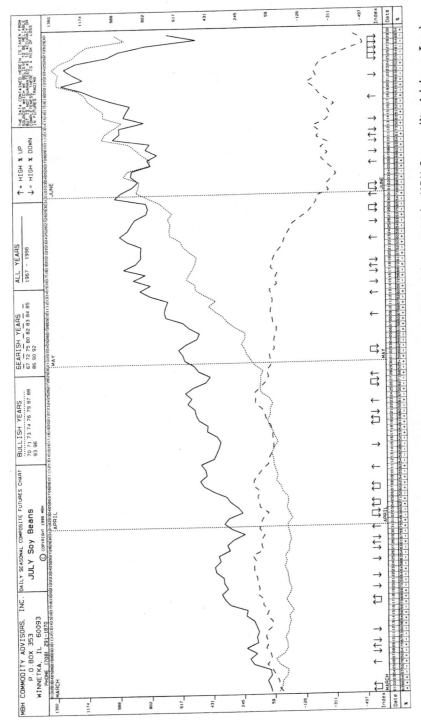

Figure A-2 Daily seasonal futures chart, July soybeans, 1967–1996. (Copyright © 1996 by MBH Commodity Advisors, Inc.)

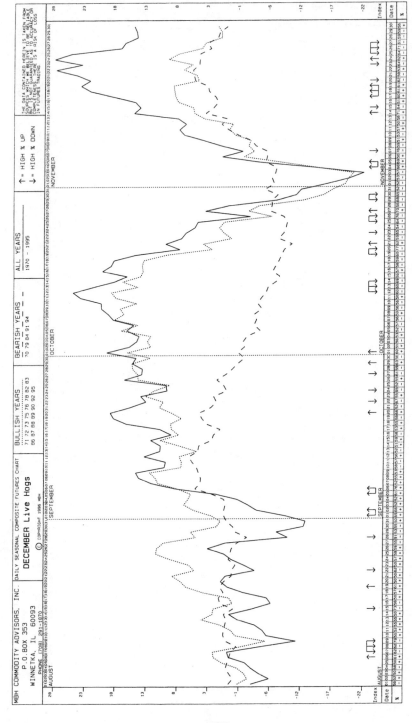

Figure A-3 Daily seasonal futures chart, December live hogs, 1970–1995. (Copyright © 1996 by MBH Commodity Advisors, Inc.)

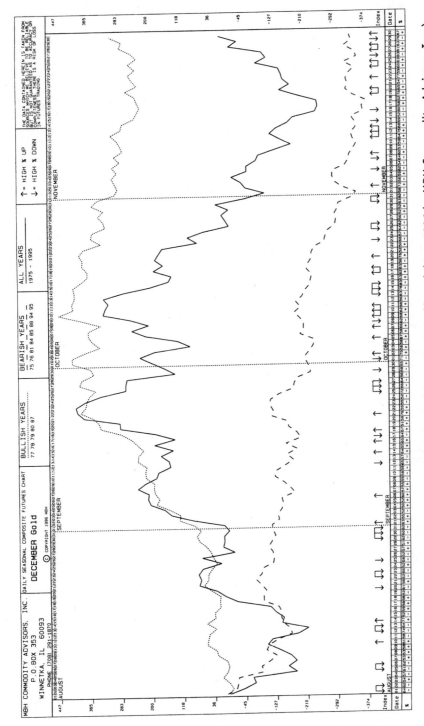

Figure A-4 Daily seasonal futures chart, December gold, 1975–1995. (Copyright © 1996 by MBH Commodity Advisors, Inc.)

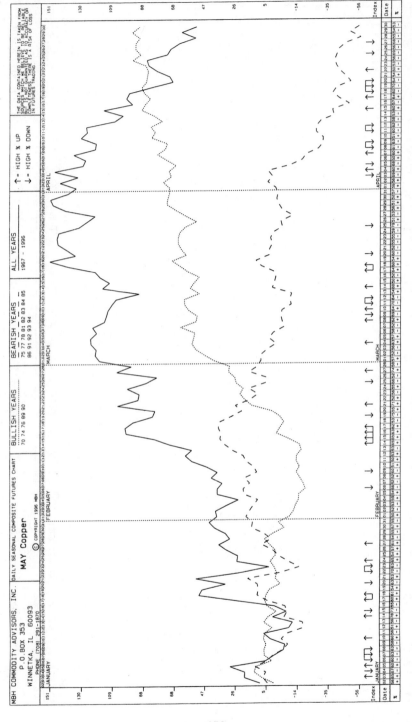

Figure A-5 Daily seasonal futures chart, May copper, 1967–1996. (Copyright © 1996 by MBH Commodity Advisors, Inc.)

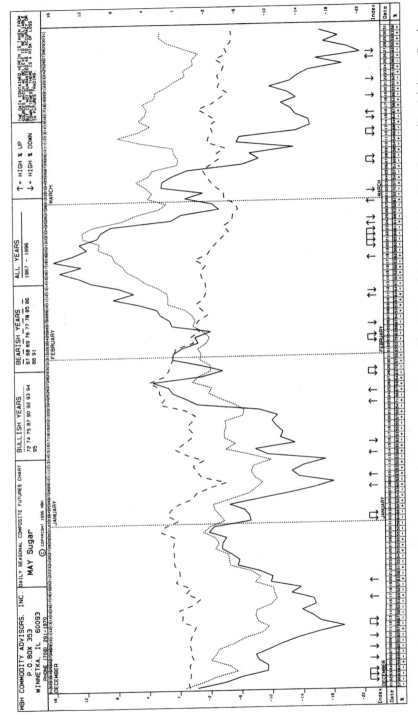

Figure A-6 Daily seasonal futures chart, May sugar, 1967–1996. (Copyright © 1996 by MBH Commodity Advisors, Inc.)

159

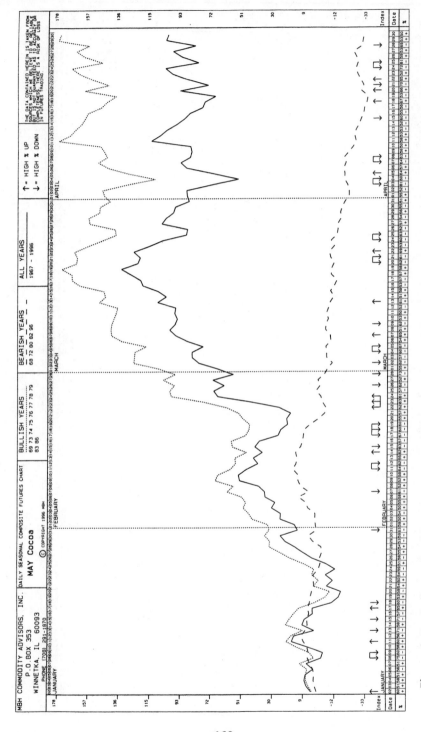

Figure A-7 Daily seasonal futures chart, May cocoa, 1967–1996. (Copyright © 1996 by MBH Commodity Advisors, Inc.)

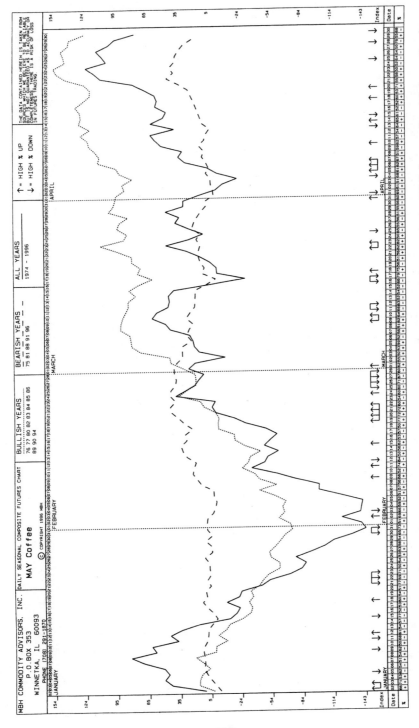

Figure A-8 Daily seasonal futures chart, May coffee, 1974–1996. (Copyright © 1996 by MBH Commodity Advisors, Inc.)

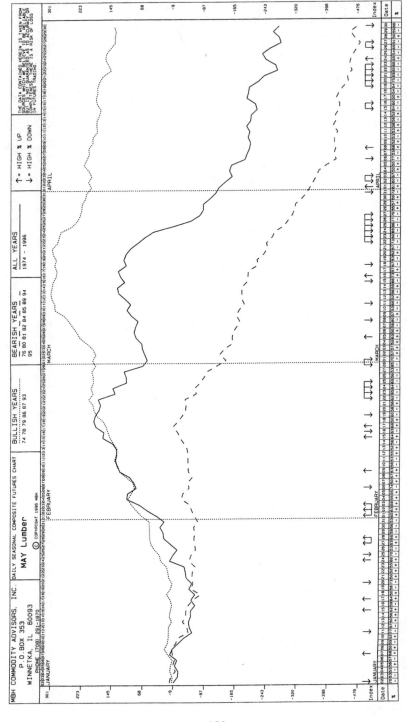

Figure A-9 Daily seasonal futures chart, May lumber, 1974–1996. (Copyright © 1996 by MBH Commodity Advisors, Inc.)

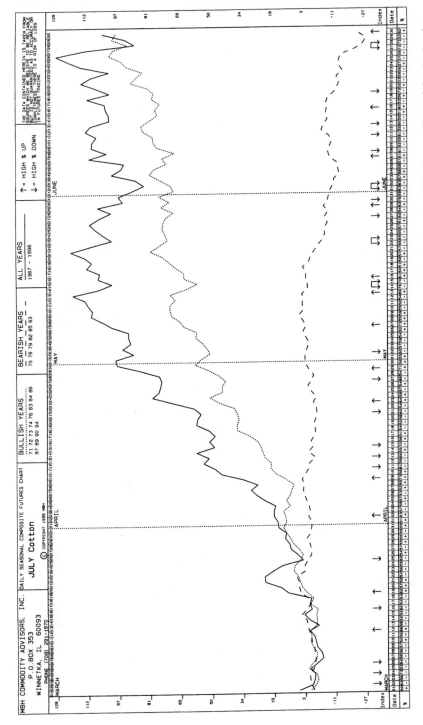

Figure A-10 Daily seasonal futures chart, July cotton, 1967–1996. (Copyright © 1996 by MBH Commodity Advisors, Inc.)

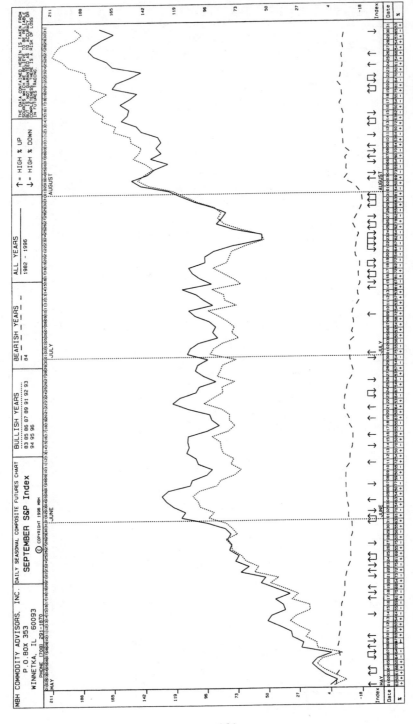

Figure A-11 Daily seasonal futures chart, September Standard & Poor's, 1982–1996. (Copyright © 1996 by MBH Commodity Advisors, Inc.)

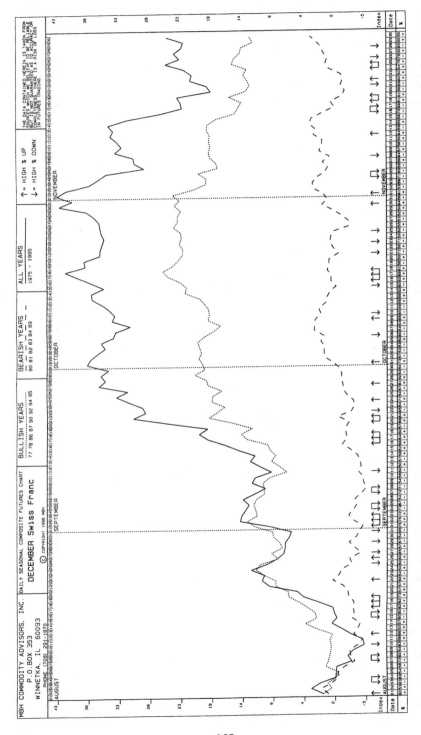

Figure A-12 Daily seasonal futures chart, December Swiss franc, 1975–1995. (Copyright © 1996 by MBH Commodity Advisors, Inc.)

165

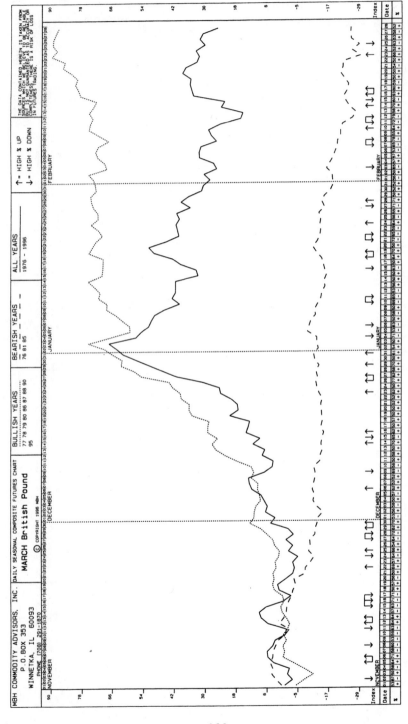

Figure A-13 Daily seasonal futures chart, March British pound, 1976–1996. (Copyright © 1996 by MBH Commodity Advisors, Inc.)

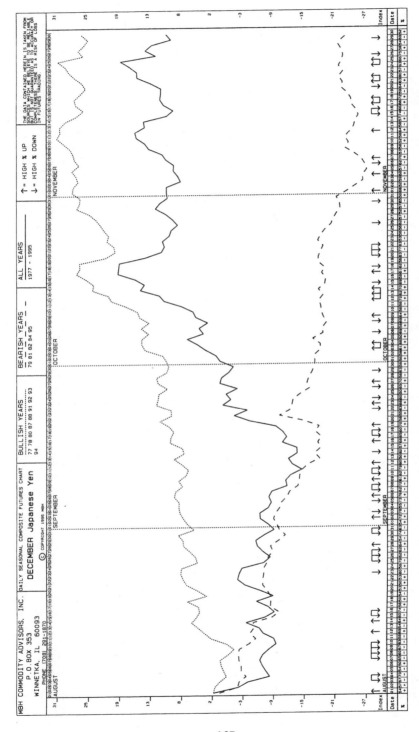

Figure A-14 Daily seasonal futures chart, December Japanese yen, 1977–1995. (Copyright © 1996 by MBH Commodity Advisors, Inc.)

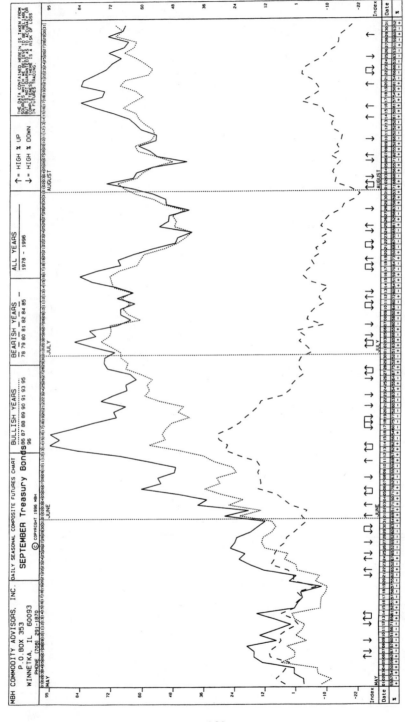

Figure A-15 Daily seasonal futures chart, September T-bonds, 1976–1996. (Copyright © 1996 by MBH Commodity Advisors, Inc.)

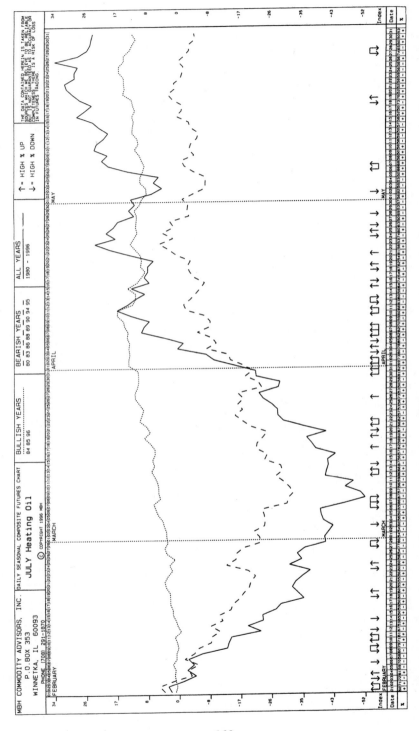

Figure A-16 Daily seasonal futures chart, July heating oil, 1980–1996. (Copyright © 1996 by MBH Commodity Advisors, Inc.)

169

APPENDIX B

MONTHLY SEASONAL CASH CHARTS

The charts in this appendix (Figures B-1 through B-16) will remain reasonably current for perhaps several more years. However, as time passes, seasonal tendencies change—some becoming stronger, some weaker. If you regularly use and follow seasonal price patterns in your marketing, hedging, or speculating programs, be sure you use up-to-date information.

WHEAT

Overall reliability of the wheat market (see Figure B-1) on a seasonal cash basis is high; the strong year-end uptrend is the most reliable and ordinarily lasts from July through November. This uptrend contains all of the high-profitability moves in the wheat market with the exception of the May–June decline. The balance of the reliabilities is too low to be useful in trading.

SOYBEANS

The cash trends in soybean prices (see Figure B-2) are self-explanatory. Although a fairly long database was used in making the analysis, a

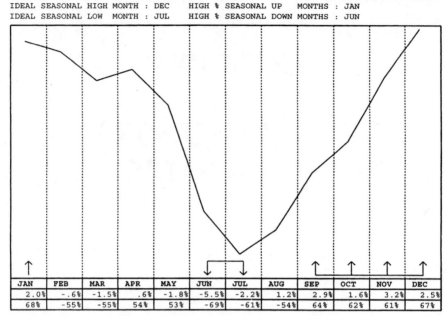

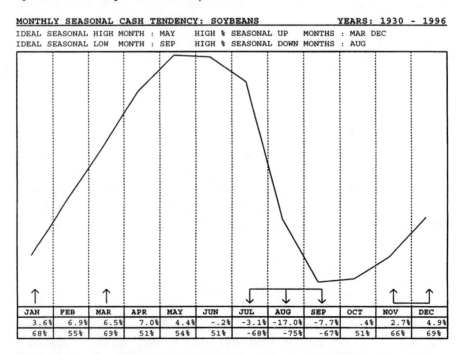

number of monthly readings stand out as reliable and useful. The traditional pattern calls for summer highs and October lows.

LIVE HOGS

The seasonal pattern in hogs (see Figure B-3) is one of my favorites. I believe that you can make more money trading the seasonal patterns in hogs than you can in virtually any other market. When combined with good timing indicators and the highly reliable short-term hog cycle, this market is an excellent speculative vehicle. Note particularly the strong seasonal tendency for upmoves late in the year and the strong probability for highs during midyear. Do not ignore this

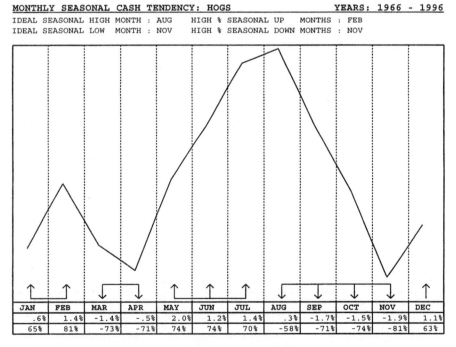

MONTHLY SEASONAL CASH TENDENCY: HOGS   YEARS: 1966 - 1996
IDEAL SEASONAL HIGH MONTH : AUG   HIGH % SEASONAL UP   MONTHS : FEB
IDEAL SEASONAL LOW MONTH : NOV   HIGH % SEASONAL DOWN MONTHS : NOV

JAN	FEB	MAR	APR	MAY	JUN	JUL	AUG	SEP	OCT	NOV	DEC
.6%	1.4%	-1.4%	-.5%	2.0%	1.2%	1.4%	.3%	-1.7%	-1.5%	-1.9%	1.1%
65%	81%	-73%	-71%	74%	74%	70%	-58%	-71%	-74%	-81%	63%

Figure B-3   Monthly cash seasonal chart, live hogs, 1966–1996. (Copyright © 1997 by MBH Commodity Advisors, Inc.)

repetitive pattern; it holds up well even in the most severe of bear markets and is a classic example of seasonality. Note also that the decline from September through November is the highest-reliability move in this market.

GOLD

The gold market (see Figure B-4) has only two seasonal moves: the drop from March to April and the downmove from December to January. Unfortunately, gold does not exhibit good seasonal tendencies on a cash basis. We will continue to monitor this market to see what changes occur in the future. Futures show a different pattern, however.

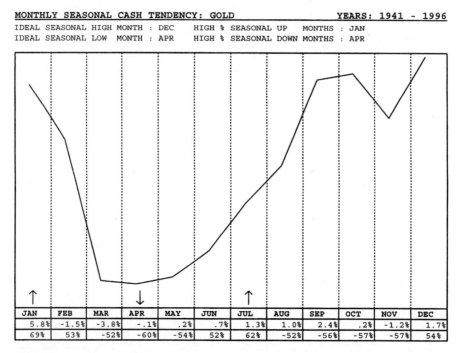

MONTHLY SEASONAL CASH TENDENCY: GOLD   YEARS: 1941 - 1996

IDEAL SEASONAL HIGH MONTH : DEC   HIGH % SEASONAL UP   MONTHS : JAN
IDEAL SEASONAL LOW MONTH : APR   HIGH % SEASONAL DOWN MONTHS : APR

JAN	FEB	MAR	APR	MAY	JUN	JUL	AUG	SEP	OCT	NOV	DEC
5.8%	-1.5%	-3.8%	-.1%	.2%	.7%	1.3%	1.0%	2.4%	.2%	-1.2%	1.7%
69%	53%	-52%	-60%	-54%	52%	62%	-52%	-56%	-57%	-57%	54%

Figure B-4   Monthly cash seasonal chart, gold, 1941–1996. (Copyright © 1997 by MBH Commodity Advisors, Inc.)

COPPER

Copper reliabilities are somewhat deceptive (see Figure B-5). For many years, prices did not show much movement from month to month. More recently, copper has been in a rather wide trading range. It has also been in a big bull market with a large bear on its heels. Consequently, some of the seasonal month-to-month patterns are deceptively high or low. Take these figures with more caution than you normally would. Remember, however, that once copper prices get going in a given direction, the resulting move is usually big. The strong seasonal upmoves in this market come in February–March and December–January. Look for highs early in the year.

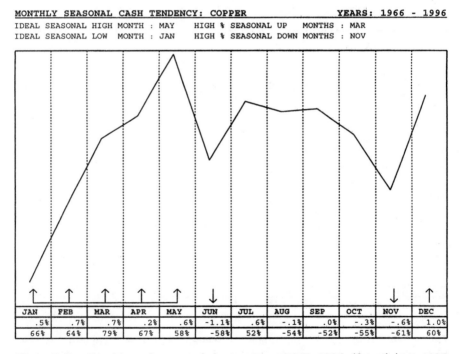

MONTHLY SEASONAL CASH TENDENCY: COPPER	YEARS: 1966 - 1996

IDEAL SEASONAL HIGH MONTH : MAY   HIGH % SEASONAL UP   MONTHS : MAR
IDEAL SEASONAL LOW   MONTH : JAN   HIGH % SEASONAL DOWN MONTHS : NOV

JAN	FEB	MAR	APR	MAY	JUN	JUL	AUG	SEP	OCT	NOV	DEC
.5%	.7%	.7%	.2%	.6%	-1.1%	.6%	-.1%	.0%	-.3%	-.6%	1.0%
66%	64%	79%	67%	58%	-58%	52%	-54%	-52%	-55%	-61%	60%

Figure B-5 Monthly cash seasonal chart, copper, 1966–1996. (Copyright © 1997 by MBH Commodity Advisors, Inc.)

SUGAR

This sugar chart (see Figure B-6) differs greatly from many others I have seen, perhaps because my data probably go back much further. In any event, the market shows few reliable seasonal patterns. The strongest moves in this market are the upmoves from May–June to June–July and from August–September to September–October.

COCOA

The overall reliability of cocoa (see Figure B-7) is low. The major thing to remember in cocoa is that it is more subject to major market cycles

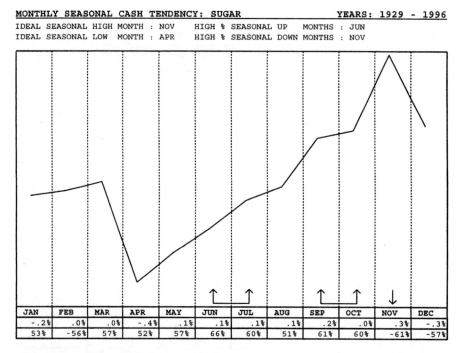

MONTHLY SEASONAL CASH TENDENCY: SUGAR   YEARS: 1929 - 1996
IDEAL SEASONAL HIGH MONTH : NOV   HIGH % SEASONAL UP   MONTHS : JUN
IDEAL SEASONAL LOW MONTH : APR   HIGH % SEASONAL DOWN MONTHS : NOV

JAN	FEB	MAR	APR	MAY	JUN	JUL	AUG	SEP	OCT	NOV	DEC
-.2%	.0%	.0%	-.4%	.1%	.1%	.1%	.1%	.2%	.0%	.3%	-.3%
53%	-56%	57%	52%	57%	66%	60%	51%	61%	60%	-61%	-57%

Figure B-6   Monthly cash seasonal chart, sugar, 1929–1996. (Copyright © 1997 by MBH Commodity Advisors, Inc.)

than seasonal ones, which accounts for the poor seasonal reliability. I am averse to trading cocoa on a seasonal basis using the cash tendency. Note that the futures tendency *does* contain some reliable patterns. Only the May–June to June–July upmove is reliable.

COFFEE

Coffee (see Figure B-8) returns have shown various strong seasonal patterns that do not appear in the cash data. Hence, the cash seasonal monthly chart for coffee may not be very helpful. I include it here for reference purposes only.

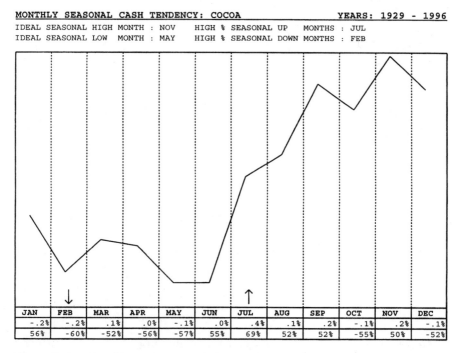

MONTHLY SEASONAL CASH TENDENCY: COCOA   YEARS: 1929 - 1996

IDEAL SEASONAL HIGH MONTH : NOV   HIGH % SEASONAL UP MONTHS : JUL
IDEAL SEASONAL LOW MONTH : MAY   HIGH % SEASONAL DOWN MONTHS : FEB

JAN	FEB	MAR	APR	MAY	JUN	JUL	AUG	SEP	OCT	NOV	DEC
-.2%	-.2%	.1%	.0%	-.1%	.0%	.4%	.1%	.2%	-.1%	.2%	-.1%
56%	-60%	-52%	-56%	-57%	55%	69%	52%	52%	-55%	50%	-52%

Figure B-7 Monthly cash seasonal chart, cocoa, 1929–1996. (Copyright © 1997 by MBH Commodity Advisors, Inc.)

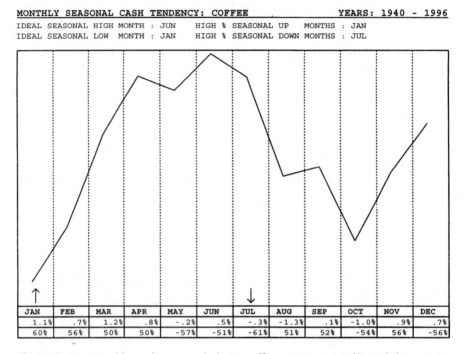

Figure B-8   Monthly cash seasonal chart, coffee, 1940–1996. (Copyright © 1997 by MBH Commodity Advisors, Inc.)

LUMBER

The lumber market (see Figure B-9) exhibits two major seasonal trends: the upmove from the beginning of the year to March and the decline from September to November. Look for seasonal highs in September.

COTTON

Cotton (see Figure B-10) is a good trend market, and once patterns change, they usually stick for many months. This points up the necessity of knowing longer-term cycles in cotton. Generally however, it is reasonable to expect highs in the June–July period following a reliable upmove from the beginning of the year.

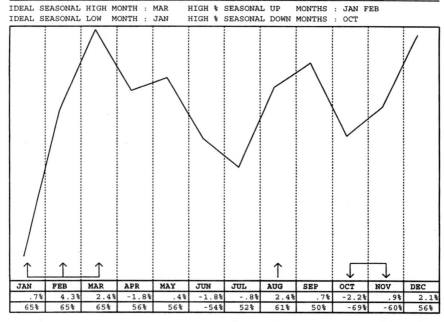

IDEAL SEASONAL HIGH MONTH : MAR   HIGH % SEASONAL UP   MONTHS : JAN FEB
IDEAL SEASONAL LOW MONTH : JAN   HIGH % SEASONAL DOWN MONTHS : OCT

JAN	FEB	MAR	APR	MAY	JUN	JUL	AUG	SEP	OCT	NOV	DEC
.7%	4.3%	2.4%	-1.8%	.4%	-1.8%	-.8%	2.4%	.7%	-2.2%	.9%	2.1%
65%	65%	65%	56%	56%	-54%	52%	61%	50%	-69%	-60%	56%

Figure B-9 Monthly cash seasonal chart, lumber, 1938–1996. (Copyright ©
1997 by MBH Commodity Advisors, Inc.)

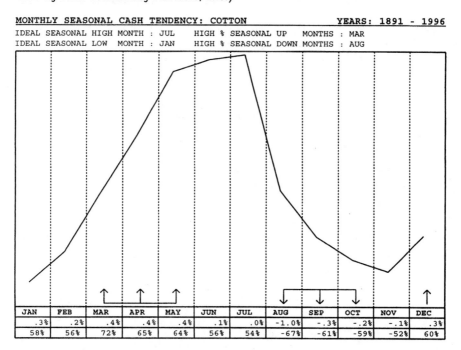

IDEAL SEASONAL HIGH MONTH : JUL   HIGH % SEASONAL UP   MONTHS : MAR
IDEAL SEASONAL LOW MONTH : JAN   HIGH % SEASONAL DOWN MONTHS : AUG

JAN	FEB	MAR	APR	MAY	JUN	JUL	AUG	SEP	OCT	NOV	DEC
.3%	.2%	.4%	.4%	.4%	.1%	.0%	-1.0%	-.3%	-.2%	-.1%	.3%
58%	56%	72%	65%	64%	56%	54%	-67%	-61%	-59%	-52%	60%

Figure B-10 Monthly cash seasonal chart, cotton, 1891–1996. (Copyright ©
1997 by MBH Commodity Advisors, Inc.)

MONTHLY SEASONAL CASH TENDENCY: SP   YEARS: 1940 - 1995

IDEAL SEASONAL HIGH MONTH : DEC   HIGH % SEASONAL UP   MONTHS : JAN
IDEAL SEASONAL LOW MONTH : JAN   HIGH % SEASONAL DOWN MONTHS : NONE

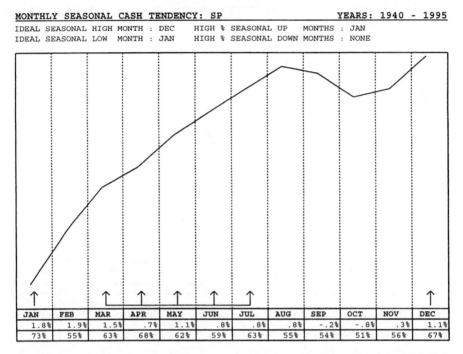

JAN	FEB	MAR	APR	MAY	JUN	JUL	AUG	SEP	OCT	NOV	DEC
1.8%	1.9%	1.5%	.7%	1.1%	.8%	.8%	.8%	-.2%	-.8%	.3%	1.1%
73%	55%	63%	68%	62%	59%	63%	55%	54%	51%	56%	67%

Figure B-11   Monthly cash seasonal chart, Standard & Poor's, 1940–1995. (Copyright © 1997 by MBH Commodity Advisors, Inc.)

STANDARD & POOR'S

The Standard & Poor's (S&P) index (see Figure B-11) is not particularly reliable on a seasonal basis. The March–April upmove is a strong one, as is the rally from November to year-end. Highs should be expected near year-end.

The Dow-Jones Industrial Average chart, as expected, correlates very closely with the S&P chart. The only reliable move that occurs in this market is the upmove from October to January.

MONTHLY SEASONAL CASH TENDENCY: SWISSFR   YEARS: 1913 - 1996

IDEAL SEASONAL HIGH MONTH : DEC   HIGH % SEASONAL UP   MONTHS : JUN
IDEAL SEASONAL LOW   MONTH : MAR   HIGH % SEASONAL DOWN MONTHS : JAN

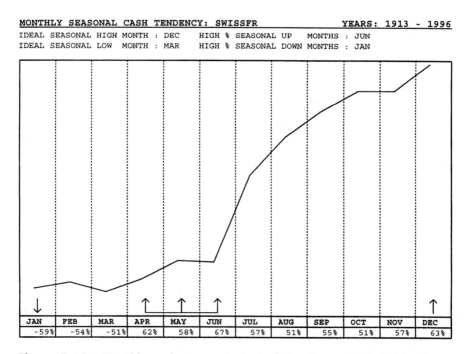

JAN	FEB	MAR	APR	MAY	JUN	JUL	AUG	SEP	OCT	NOV	DEC
-59%	-54%	-51%	62%	58%	67%	57%	51%	55%	51%	57%	63%

Figure B-12   Monthly cash seasonal chart, Swiss franc, 1913–1996. (Copyright © 1997 by MBH Commodity Advisors, Inc.)

SWISS FRANC

The Swiss franc (see Figure B-12) upmove from April to June is a strong and reliable one—and the only sustained seasonal move in this market. The November–December upmove and the December–January downmove have good reliability but are of shorter duration.

BRITISH POUND

In general, the British pound (see Figure B-13) does not seem to be a highly seasonal market. There is, however, a significant downmove from April to September. The reliability of this move makes it one that should be watched carefully.

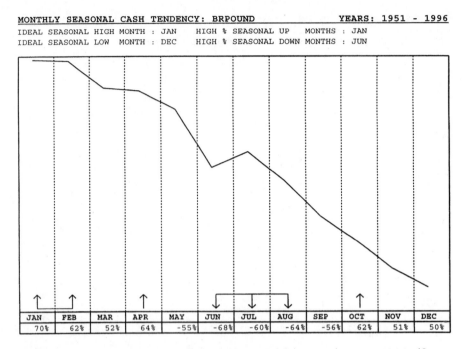

MONTHLY SEASONAL CASH TENDENCY: BRPOUND   YEARS: 1951 - 1996

IDEAL SEASONAL HIGH MONTH : JAN   HIGH % SEASONAL UP   MONTHS : JAN
IDEAL SEASONAL LOW MONTH : DEC   HIGH % SEASONAL DOWN MONTHS : JUN

JAN	FEB	MAR	APR	MAY	JUN	JUL	AUG	SEP	OCT	NOV	DEC
70%	62%	52%	64%	-55%	-68%	-60%	-64%	-56%	62%	51%	50%

Figure B-13 Monthly cash seasonal chart, British pound, 1951–1996. (Copyright © 1997 by MBH Commodity Advisors, Inc.)

JAPANESE YEN

The Japanese yen (see Figure B-14) has a fairly reliable seasonal up-move from May to September–October and a more reliable one from December to February.

T-BOND YIELDS

The T-bond market (see Figure B-15) has not been a seasonally reliable one. There are no moves that have a reliability of 65 or more. The up-move from June to August may be considered marginally reliable.

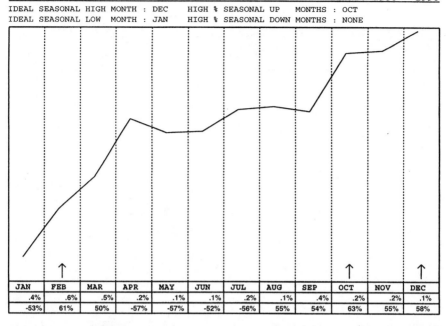

MONTHLY SEASONAL CASH TENDENCY: YEN   YEARS: 1958 - 1996
IDEAL SEASONAL HIGH MONTH : DEC   HIGH % SEASONAL UP   MONTHS : OCT
IDEAL SEASONAL LOW MONTH : JAN   HIGH % SEASONAL DOWN MONTHS : NONE

JAN	FEB	MAR	APR	MAY	JUN	JUL	AUG	SEP	OCT	NOV	DEC
.4%	.6%	.5%	.2%	.1%	.1%	.2%	.1%	.4%	.2%	.2%	.1%
-53%	61%	50%	-57%	-57%	-52%	-56%	55%	54%	63%	55%	58%

Figure B-14   Monthly cash seasonal chart, Japanese yen, 1958–1996. (Copyright © 1997 by MBH Commodity Advisors, Inc.)

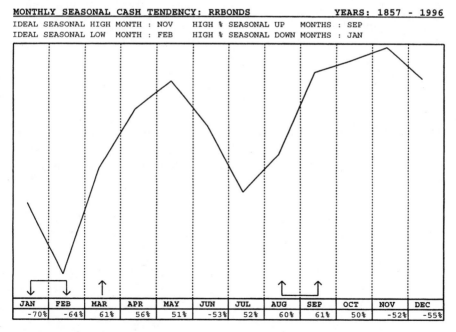

MONTHLY SEASONAL CASH TENDENCY: RRBONDS   YEARS: 1857 - 1996
IDEAL SEASONAL HIGH MONTH : NOV   HIGH % SEASONAL UP   MONTHS : SEP
IDEAL SEASONAL LOW MONTH : FEB   HIGH % SEASONAL DOWN MONTHS : JAN

JAN	FEB	MAR	APR	MAY	JUN	JUL	AUG	SEP	OCT	NOV	DEC
-70%	-64%	61%	56%	51%	-53%	52%	60%	61%	50%	-52%	-55%

Figure B-15   Monthly cash seasonal chart, T-bond yields, 1857–1996. (Copyright © 1997 by MBH Commodity Advisors, Inc.)

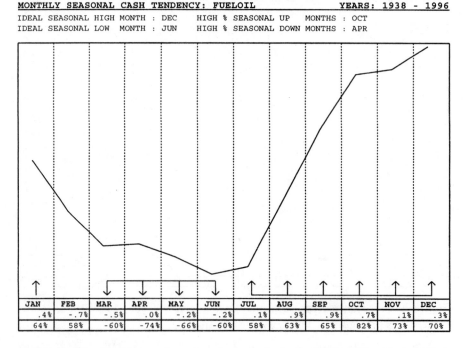

	JAN	FEB	MAR	APR	MAY	JUN	JUL	AUG	SEP	OCT	NOV	DEC
	.4%	-.7%	-.5%	.0%	-.2%	-.2%	.1%	.9%	.9%	.7%	.1%	.3%
	64%	58%	-60%	-74%	-66%	-60%	58%	63%	65%	82%	73%	70%

MONTHLY SEASONAL CASH TENDENCY: FUELOIL   YEARS: 1938 - 1996
IDEAL SEASONAL HIGH MONTH : DEC   HIGH % SEASONAL UP   MONTHS : OCT
IDEAL SEASONAL LOW MONTH : JUN   HIGH % SEASONAL DOWN MONTHS : APR

Figure B-16   Monthly cash seasonal chart, fuel oil, 1938–1996. (Copyright ©
1997 by MBH Commodity Advisors, Inc.)

FUEL OIL

The fuel oil market (see Figure B-16) exhibits an exceptionally strong
upmove from July to January. This is one of the most sustained and reliable moves in all the markets studied in this book. Look for highs in
December–January and lows in June–July.

APPENDIX C

SELECTED WEEKLY
SEASONAL CHARTS

Figures C-1 through C-22 show weekly seasonal futures charts for selected futures contracts and delivery months. The data used in preparing these charts are shown at the top of each chart.

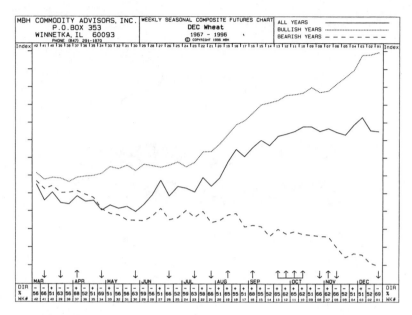

Figure C-1 Weekly seasonal composite futures chart, December wheat, 1967–1996. (Copyright © 1996 by MBH Commodity Advisors, Inc.)

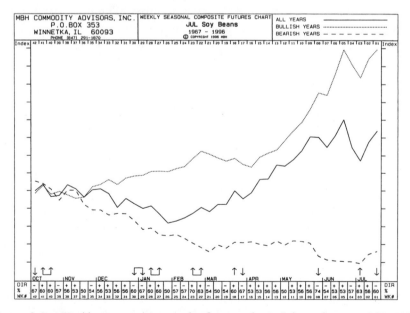

Figure C-2 Weekly seasonal composite futures chart, July soybeans, 1967–1996. (Copyright © 1996 by MBH Commodity Advisors, Inc.)

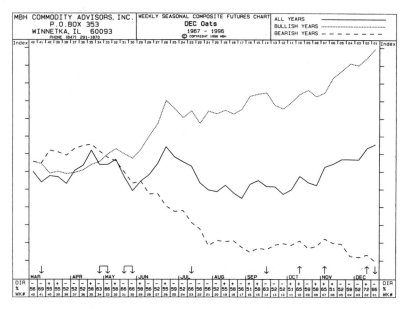

Figure C-3 Weekly seasonal composite futures chart, December oats, 1967–1996. (Copyright © 1996 by MBH Commodity Advisors, Inc.)

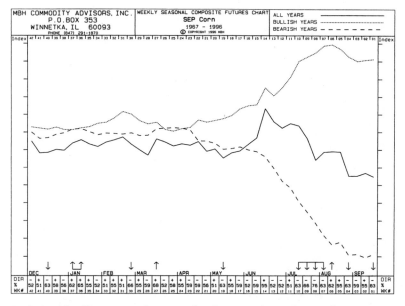

Figure C-4 Weekly seasonal composite futures chart, September corn, 1967–1996. (Copyright © 1996 by MBH Commodity Advisors, Inc.)

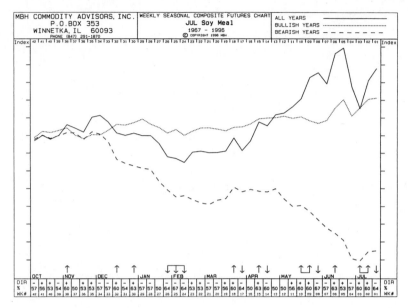

Figure C-5   Weekly seasonal composite futures chart, July soybean meal, 1967–1996. (Copyright © 1996 by MBH Commodity Advisors, Inc.)

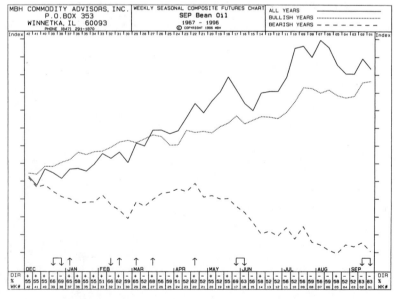

Figure C-6   Weekly seasonal composite futures chart, September soybean oil, 1967–1996. (Copyright © 1996 by MBH Commodity Advisors, Inc.)

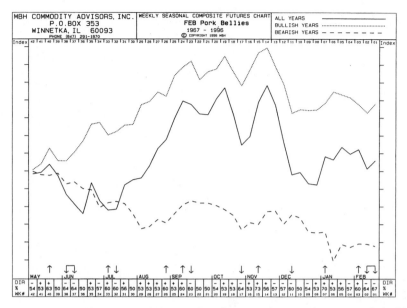

Figure C-7 Weekly seasonal composite futures chart, February pork bellies, 1967–1996. (Copyright © 1996 by MBH Commodity Advisors, Inc.)

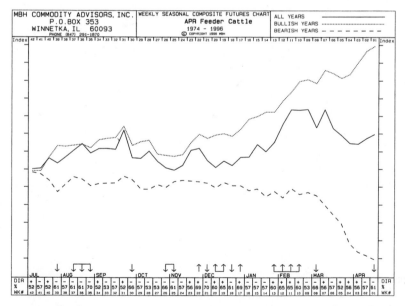

Figure C-8 Weekly seasonal composite futures chart, April feeder cattle, 1974–1996. (Copyright © 1996 by MBH Commodity Advisors, Inc.)

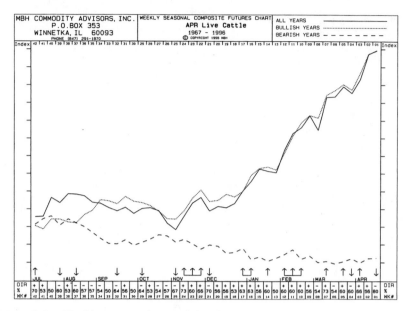

Figure C-9 Weekly seasonal composite futures chart, April live cattle, 1967–1996. (Copyright © 1996 by MBH Commodity Advisors, Inc.)

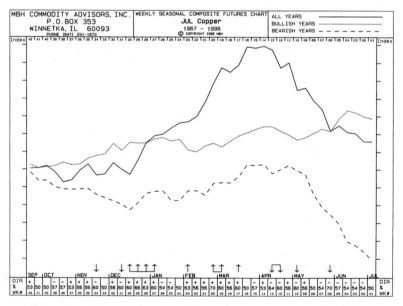

Figure C-10 Weekly seasonal composite futures chart, July copper, 1967–1996. (Copyright © 1996 by MBH Commodity Advisors, Inc.)

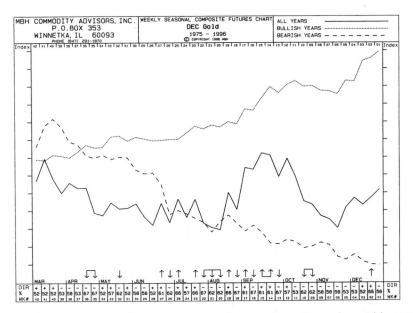

Figure C-11 Weekly seasonal composite futures chart, December gold, 1975–1996. (Copyright © 1996 by MBH Commodity Advisors, Inc.)

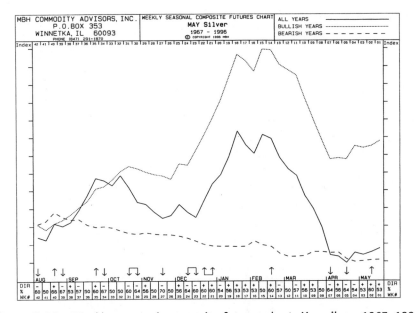

Figure C-12 Weekly seasonal composite futures chart, May silver, 1967–1996. (Copyright © 1996 by MBH Commodity Advisors, Inc.)

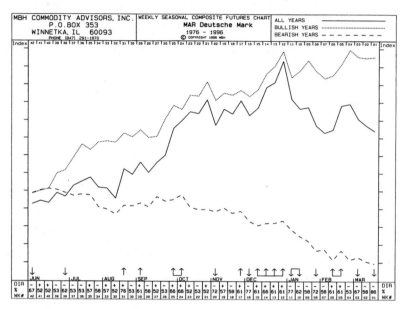

Figure C-13 Weekly seasonal composite futures chart, December deutsche marks, 1976–1996. (Copyright © 1996 by MBH Commodity Advisors, Inc.)

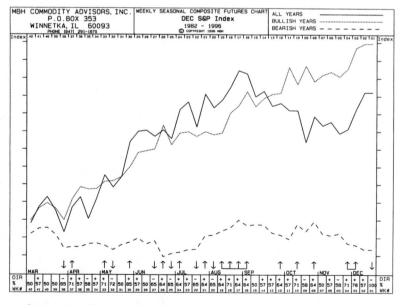

Figure C-14 Weekly seasonal composite futures chart, December Standard & Poor's, 500, 1982–1996. (Copyright © 1996 by MBH Commodity Advisors, Inc.)

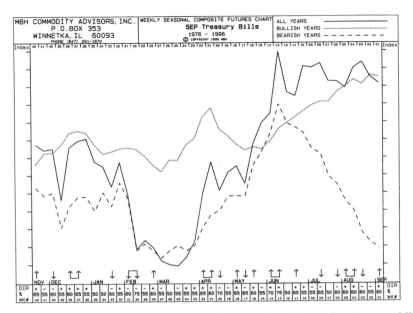

Figure C-15 Weekly seasonal composite futures chart, September Treasury bills, 1976–1996. (Copyright © 1996 by MBH Commodity Advisors, Inc.)

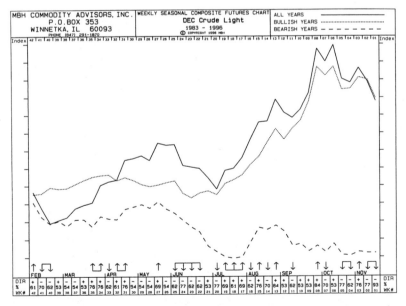

Figure C-16 Weekly seasonal composite futures chart, December crude oil, 1983–1996. (Copyright © 1996 by MBH Commodity Advisors, Inc.)

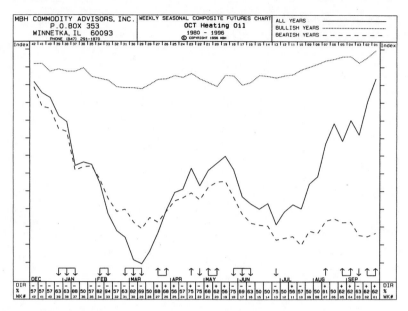

Figure C-17 Weekly seasonal composite futures chart, October heating oil, 1980–1996. (Copyright © 1996 by MBH Commodity Advisors, Inc.)

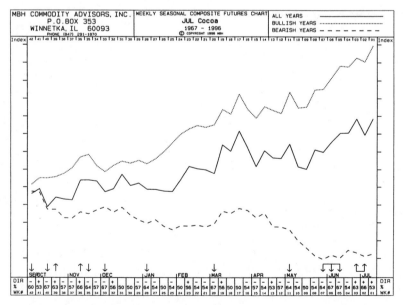

Figure C-18 Weekly seasonal composite futures chart, July cocoa, 1967–1996. (Copyright © 1996 by MBH Commodity Advisors, Inc.)

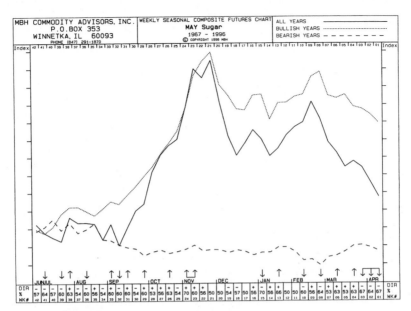

Figure C-19 Weekly seasonal composite futures chart, May sugar, 1967–1996. (Copyright © 1996 by MBH Commodity Advisors, Inc.)

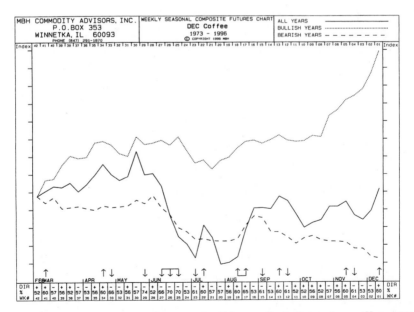

Figure C-20 Weekly seasonal composite futures chart, December coffee, 1973–1996. (Copyright © 1996 by MBH Commodity Advisors, Inc.)

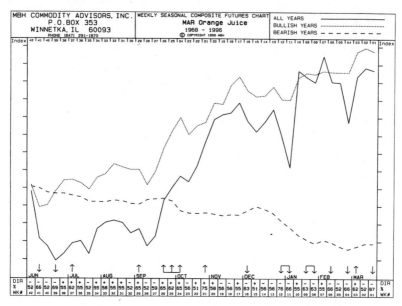

Figure C-21 Weekly seasonal composite futures chart, March orange juice, 1968–1996. (Copyright © 1996 by MBH Commodity Advisors, Inc.)

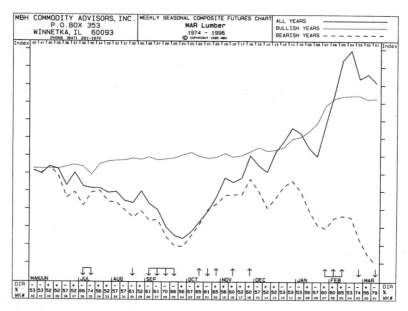

Figure C-22 Weekly seasonal composite futures chart, March lumber, 1974–1996. (Copyright © 1996 by MBH Commodity Advisors, Inc.)

APPENDIX D

KEY DATE SEASONAL TRADES

This appendix contains a selection of key date seasonal trades (Tables D-1 through D-11). I have chosen several trades from each major market to illustrate how the key date seasonals have worked in the past. Refer to Chapter 8 for specific instructions on how to read the seasonal listing tables. You should assume that the future performance of seasonal trades will equal or exceed past results. Although the information contained in these tables has been obtained from sources I believe are reliable, I cannot guarantee their accuracy or completeness. Do not assume that you will profit—or have losses—from seasonal commodity trades.

TABLE D-1   Long July Live Hogs
(Enter: 1/18; Exit: 1/28; Stop: 4; P/L Ratio: 3.19)

Year	Date In	Price In	Date Out	Price Out	Profit/Loss	Total
1970	1/19/70	27.350	1/28/70	27.450	0.100	0.100
1971	1/18/71	19.800	1/28/71	20.550	0.750	0.850
1972	1/18/72	27.600	1/28/72	28.170	0.570	1.420
1973	1/18/73	31.870	1/29/73	32.270	0.400	1.820
1974	1/18/74	48.050	1/28/74	48.950	0.900	2.720
1975	1/20/75	42.750	1/28/75	44.720	1.970	4.690
1976	1/19/76	46.600	1/21/76	43.600	−3.000	1.690
1977	1/18/77	36.600	1/28/77	37.870	1.270	2.960
1978	1/18/78	40.670	1/30/78	42.770	2.100	5.060
1979	1/18/79	50.270	1/29/79	52.770	2.500	7.560
1980	1/18/80	43.770	1/28/80	44.070	0.300	7.860
1981	1/19/81	52.150	1/28/81	53.550	1.400	9.260
1982	1/18/82	49.700	1/28/82	51.800	2.100	11.360
1983	1/18/83	56.820	1/28/83	55.670	−1.150	10.210
1984	1/18/84	56.120	1/30/84	55.270	−0.850	9.360
1985	1/18/85	54.370	1/28/85	54.470	0.100	9.460
1986	1/20/86	46.100	1/28/86	46.820	0.720	10.180
1987	1/19/87	45.500	1/28/87	46.900	1.400	11.580
1988	1/18/88	49.200	1/28/88	47.950	−1.250	10.330
1989	1/18/89	48.250	1/30/89	47.520	−0.730	9.600
1990	1/18/90	52.820	1/29/90	52.850	0.030	9.630
1991	1/18/91	54.500	1/28/91	55.570	1.070	10.700
1992	1/20/92	43.870	1/28/92	44.470	0.600	11.300
1993	1/18/93	47.370	1/28/93	47.550	0.180	11.480
1994	1/18/94	53.250	1/28/94	54.900	1.650	13.130
1995	1/18/95	45.070	1/30/95	45.050	−0.020	13.110
1996	1/18/96	49.020	1/29/96	49.320	0.300	13.410
1997	1/20/97	76.650	1/28/97	78.550	1.900	15.310

Trades: 28   Average Profit: 1.01

Winners: 22   Average Loss: −1.17

Losers: 6   % Average Profit: 2.27

% Winners: 78.57   % Average Loss: −2.35

Note: There is a risk of loss in futures trading.

TABLE D-2 Long March Coffee
(Enter: 1/30; Exit: 2/5; Stop: 3; P/L Ratio: 5.56)

Year	Date In	Price In	Date Out	Price Out	Profit/Loss	Total
1974	1/30/74	73.280	2/5/74	75.500	2.220	2.220
1975	1/30/75	55.200	2/5/75	53.960	−1.240	0.980
1976	1/30/76	95.000	2/5/76	98.950	3.950	4.930
1977	1/31/77	222.930	2/7/77	235.900	12.970	17.900
1978	1/30/78	192.000	2/6/78	194.250	2.250	20.150
1979	1/30/79	124.800	2/5/79	127.750	2.950	23.100
1980	1/30/80	165.000	2/5/80	166.000	1.000	24.100
1981	1/30/81	122.360	2/4/81	116.580	−5.780	18.320
1982	2/1/82	148.680	2/5/82	150.480	1.800	20.120
1983	1/31/83	122.810	2/7/83	126.560	3.750	23.870
1984	1/30/84	142.610	2/6/84	142.770	0.160	24.030
1985	1/30/85	147.630	2/5/85	152.040	4.410	28.440
1986	1/30/86	207.590	2/5/86	226.120	18.520	46.970
1987	1/30/87	123.980	2/5/87	125.910	1.930	48.900
1988	2/1/88	133.380	2/5/88	136.700	3.320	52.220
1989	1/30/89	136.010	2/6/89	138.000	1.990	54.210
1990	1/30/90	80.370	2/5/90	80.040	−0.330	53.880
1991	1/30/91	82.950	2/5/91	84.350	1.400	55.280
1992	1/30/92	74.600	1/31/92	72.150	−2.450	52.830
1993	2/1/93	60.950	2/5/93	62.600	1.650	54.480
1994	1/31/94	72.350	2/7/94	76.900	4.550	59.030
1995	1/30/95	157.450	2/6/95	153.900	−3.550	55.480
1996	1/30/96	119.550	2/5/96	120.650	1.100	56.580
1997	1/30/97	140.300	2/5/97	144.550	4.250	60.830

Trades: 24	Average Profit: 3.90
Winners: 19	Average Loss: −2.67
Losers: 5	% Average Profit: 2.82
% Winners: 79.17	% Average Loss: −2.58

Note: There is a risk of loss in futures trading.

TABLE D-3   Long May Cotton
(Enter: 2/9; Exit: 4/14; Stop: 7; P/L Ratio: 3.26)

Year	Date In	Price In	Date Out	Price Out	Profit/Loss	Total
1973	2/9/73	37.840	4/16/73	47.500	9.660	9.660
1974	2/11/74	77.570	2/15/74	70.320	−7.250	2.410
1975	2/10/75	40.120	4/14/75	43.020	2.900	5.310
1976	2/9/76	59.720	4/14/76	60.070	0.350	5.660
1977	2/9/77	76.070	4/14/77	78.370	2.300	7.960
1978	2/9/78	57.470	4/14/78	57.490	0.020	7.980
1979	2/9/79	66.900	3/7/79	62.190	−4.710	3.270
1980	2/11/80	88.840	2/22/80	81.980	−6.860	−3.590
1981	2/9/81	87.830	4/14/81	87.700	−0.130	−3.720
1982	2/9/82	65.630	4/14/82	66.100	0.470	−3.250
1983	2/9/83	66.270	4/14/83	70.670	4.400	1.150
1984	2/9/84	74.870	4/16/84	78.480	3.610	4.760
1985	2/11/85	66.410	4/15/85	68.370	1.960	6.720
1986	2/10/86	60.580	4/14/86	62.250	1.670	8.390
1987	2/9/87	55.120	4/14/87	61.950	6.830	15.220
1988	2/9/88	62.250	4/14/88	62.950	0.700	15.920
1989	2/9/89	58.190	4/14/89	64.490	6.300	22.220
1990	2/9/90	68.150	4/16/90	74.070	5.920	28.140
1991	2/11/91	82.040	4/15/91	87.850	5.810	33.950
1992	2/10/92	56.070	4/15/92	56.980	0.910	34.860
1993	2/9/93	61.150	4/14/93	62.850	1.700	36.560
1994	2/9/94	76.850	4/14/94	81.270	4.420	40.980
1995	2/9/95	89.850	4/17/95	110.220	20.370	61.350
1996	2/9/96	86.100	4/15/96	83.890	−2.210	59.140
1997	2/10/97	75.860	4/14/97	72.360	−3.500	55.640

Trades: 25	Average Profit: 4.23
Winners: 19	Average Loss: −4.11
Losers: 6	% Average Profit: 6.70
% Winners: 76.00	% Average Loss: −5.24

Note: There is a risk of loss in futures trading.

TABLE D-4   Short May Wheat
(Enter: 3/9; Exit: 3/13; Stop: 7; P/L Ratio: 3.35)

Year	Date In	Price In	Date Out	Price Out	Profit/Loss	Total
1969	3/10/69	132.625	3/13/69	132.250	0.375	0.375
1970	3/9/70	145.125	3/13/70	147.125	−2.000	−1.625
1971	3/9/71	163.000	3/15/71	161.750	1.250	−0.375
1972	3/9/72	157.875	3/13/72	157.375	0.500	0.125
1973	3/9/73	234.375	3/13/73	217.750	16.625	16.750
1974	3/11/74	523.500	3/13/74	532.500	−9.000	7.750
1975	3/10/75	354.750	3/13/75	362.500	−7.750	0.000
1976	3/9/76	381.250	3/15/76	370.750	10.500	10.500
1977	3/9/77	283.750	3/14/77	277.250	6.500	17.000
1978	3/9/78	280.250	3/13/78	283.750	−3.500	13.500
1979	3/9/79	354.000	3/13/79	338.250	15.750	29.250
1980	3/10/80	439.000	3/13/80	435.250	3.750	33.000
1981	3/9/81	437.250	3/13/81	437.000	0.250	33.250
1982	3/9/82	360.000	3/15/82	352.750	7.250	40.500
1983	3/9/83	328.250	3/14/83	330.250	−2.000	38.500
1984	3/9/84	354.500	3/13/84	348.000	6.500	45.000
1985	3/11/85	339.750	3/13/85	338.000	1.750	46.750
1986	3/10/86	302.250	3/13/86	296.250	6.000	52.750
1987	3/9/87	288.500	3/13/87	282.250	6.250	59.000
1988	3/9/88	304.000	3/14/88	302.750	1.250	60.250
1989	3/9/89	435.500	3/13/89	441.750	−6.250	54.000
1990	3/9/90	353.750	3/13/90	348.750	5.000	59.000
1991	3/11/91	280.500	3/13/91	288.250	−7.750	51.250
1992	3/9/92	403.250	3/13/92	385.000	18.250	69.500
1993	3/9/93	331.500	3/15/93	327.750	3.750	73.250
1994	3/9/94	336.000	3/14/94	334.750	1.250	74.500
1995	3/9/95	350.000	3/13/95	342.750	7.250	81.750
1996	3/11/96	491.500	3/13/96	484.500	7.000	88.750
1997	3/10/97	379.250	3/13/97	378.000	1.250	90.000

Trades: 29   Average Profit: 5.83
Winners: 22   Average Loss: −5.46
Losers: 7   % Average Profit: 1.78
% Winners: 75.86   % Average Loss: −1.62

Note: There is a risk of loss in futures trading.

TABLE D-5   Long September Heating Oil
(Enter: 3/29; Exit: 4/10; Stop: 2; P/L Ratio: 6.93)

Year	Date In	Price In	Date Out	Price Out	Profit/Loss	Total
1980	3/31/80	80.750	4/10/80	83.700	2.950	2.950
1981	3/30/81	100.000	4/10/81	100.680	0.680	3.630
1982	3/29/82	76.000	4/12/82	86.680	10.680	14.310
1983	3/29/83	75.900	4/11/83	79.800	3.900	18.210
1984	3/29/84	79.700	4/10/84	80.000	0.300	18.510
1985	3/29/85	73.600	4/10/85	75.800	2.200	20.710
1986	3/31/86	34.600	4/10/86	39.700	5.100	25.810
1987	3/30/87	49.700	4/9/87	48.680	−1.020	24.790
1988	3/29/88	45.700	4/11/88	47.260	1.560	26.350
1989	3/29/89	51.500	4/5/89	49.580	−1.920	24.430
1990	3/29/90	54.630	4/9/90	53.290	−1.340	23.090
1991	4/1/91	54.010	4/10/91	56.880	2.870	25.960
1992	3/30/92	54.780	4/10/92	57.400	2.620	28.580
1993	3/29/93	57.410	4/12/93	58.090	0.680	29.260
1994	3/29/94	44.250	4/11/94	47.790	3.540	32.800
1995	3/29/95	49.680	4/10/95	51.100	1.420	34.220
1996	3/29/96	52.470	4/10/96	53.970	1.500	35.720
1997	3/31/97	55.970	4/2/97	54.480	−1.490	34.230

Trades: 18	Average Profit: 2.86
Winners: 14	Average Loss: −1.44
Losers: 4	% Average Profit: 5.00
% Winners: 77.78	% Average Loss: −2.72

Note: There is a risk of loss in futures trading.

TABLE D-6   Short June Live Hogs
(Enter: 5/22; Exit: 5/30; Stop: 3; P/L Ratio: 2.32)

Year	Date In	Price In	Date Out	Price Out	Profit/Loss	Total
1970	5/22/70	26.820	6/1/70	26.150	0.670	0.670
1971	5/24/71	21.050	6/1/71	20.900	0.150	0.820
1972	5/22/72	28.320	5/30/72	28.120	0.200	1.020
1973	5/22/73	38.670	5/25/73	39.950	−1.280	−0.260
1974	5/22/74	29.720	5/30/74	27.020	2.700	2.440
1975	5/22/75	47.520	5/30/75	49.170	−1.650	0.790
1976	5/24/76	50.370	6/1/76	50.300	0.070	0.860
1977	5/23/77	45.470	5/31/77	45.000	0.470	1.330
1978	5/22/78	54.320	5/30/78	54.070	0.250	1.580
1979	5/22/79	45.700	5/30/79	44.970	0.730	2.310
1980	5/22/80	33.300	5/30/80	33.000	0.300	2.610
1981	5/22/81	51.220	6/1/81	51.600	−0.380	2.230
1982	5/24/82	61.850	6/1/82	61.520	0.330	2.560
1983	5/23/83	49.370	5/31/83	46.620	2.750	5.310
1984	5/22/84	53.450	5/30/84	52.100	1.350	6.660
1985	5/22/85	48.300	5/30/85	47.550	0.750	7.410
1986	5/22/86	48.300	5/28/86	50.050	−1.750	5.660
1987	5/22/87	57.100	6/1/87	59.450	−2.350	3.310
1988	5/23/88	53.620	5/31/88	54.770	−1.150	2.160
1989	5/22/89	49.050	5/30/89	47.270	1.780	3.940
1990	5/22/90	66.920	5/30/90	66.450	0.470	4.410
1991	5/22/91	56.950	5/30/91	56.900	0.050	4.460
1992	5/22/92	47.120	6/1/92	47.070	0.050	4.510
1993	5/24/93	52.870	6/1/93	51.200	1.670	6.180
1994	5/23/94	49.600	5/31/94	47.600	2.000	8.180
1995	5/22/95	43.800	5/30/95	43.350	0.450	8.630
1996	5/22/96	64.470	5/30/96	61.820	2.650	11.280

Trades: 27	Average Profit: 0.94
Winners: 21	Average Loss: −1.43
Losers: 6	% Average Profit: 2.10
% Winners: 77.78	% Average Loss: −2.90

Note: There is a risk of loss in futures trading.

TABLE D-7   Short December Wheat
(Enter: 6/21; Exit: 6/29; Stop: 5; P/L Ratio: 4.80)

Year	Date In	Price In	Date Out	Price Out	Profit/Loss	Total
1969	6/23/69	138.125	6/30/69	133.625	4.500	4.500
1970	6/22/70	144.625	6/29/70	148.875	−4.250	0.250
1971	6/21/71	166.250	6/29/71	161.500	4.750	5.000
1972	6/21/72	148.500	6/29/72	148.375	0.125	5.125
1973	6/21/73	275.250	6/29/73	267.875	7.375	12.500
1974	6/21/74	462.500	7/1/74	440.000	22.500	35.000
1975	6/23/75	335.000	6/30/75	317.750	17.250	52.250
1976	6/21/76	392.000	6/29/76	391.500	0.500	52.750
1977	6/21/77	256.250	6/29/77	264.500	−8.250	44.500
1978	6/21/78	327.500	6/29/78	318.250	9.250	53.750
1979	6/21/79	491.500	6/29/79	448.500	43.000	96.750
1980	6/23/80	457.500	6/30/80	451.500	6.000	102.750
1981	6/22/81	435.250	6/29/81	414.500	20.750	123.500
1982	6/21/82	376.250	6/29/82	378.250	−2.000	121.500
1983	6/21/83	379.250	6/29/83	370.500	8.750	130.250
1984	6/21/84	377.750	6/29/84	374.750	3.000	133.250
1985	6/21/85	332.250	7/1/85	325.750	6.500	139.750
1986	6/23/86	256.000	6/30/86	251.250	4.750	144.500
1987	6/22/87	275.750	6/29/87	270.750	5.000	149.500
1988	6/21/88	404.000	6/29/88	376.000	28.000	177.500
1989	6/21/89	418.250	6/29/89	418.750	−0.500	177.000
1990	6/21/90	353.750	6/29/90	345.500	8.250	185.250
1991	6/21/91	291.500	7/1/91	290.500	1.000	186.250
1992	6/22/92	366.250	6/29/92	364.750	1.500	187.750
1993	6/21/93	298.250	6/29/93	295.000	3.250	191.000
1994	6/21/94	342.500	6/29/94	336.250	6.250	197.250
1995	6/21/95	419.500	6/28/95	450.500	−31.000	166.250
1996	6/21/96	504.250	7/1/96	495.500	8.750	175.000

Trades: 28	Average Profit: 9.61
Winners: 23	Average Loss: −9.20
Losers: 5	% Average Profit: 2.61
% Winners: 82.14	% Average Loss: −2.84

Note: There is a risk of loss in futures trading.

TABLE D-8   Long January Platinum
(Enter: 9/16; Exit: 9/24; Stop: 4; P/L Ratio: 2.16)

Year	Date In	Price In	Date Out	Price Out	Profit/Loss	Total
1973	9/18/72	134.300	9/25/72	141.500	7.200	7.200
1974	9/17/73	169.000	9/24/73	172.500	3.500	10.700
1975	9/16/74	180.000	9/24/74	181.500	1.500	12.200
1976	9/16/75	161.700	9/23/75	154.000	−7.700	4.500
1977	9/16/76	159.000	9/24/76	167.600	8.600	13.100
1978	9/16/77	154.500	9/26/77	157.500	3.000	16.100
1979	9/18/78	267.100	9/25/78	285.900	18.800	34.900
1980	9/17/79	427.100	9/24/79	512.100	85.000	119.900
1981	9/16/80	738.800	9/24/80	759.800	21.000	140.900
1982	9/16/81	466.400	9/24/81	437.200	−29.200	111.700
1983	9/16/82	330.000	9/17/82	313.900	−16.100	95.600
1984	9/16/83	439.300	9/26/83	439.500	0.200	95.800
1985	9/17/84	327.400	9/24/84	331.700	4.300	100.100
1986	9/16/85	310.100	9/18/85	296.900	−13.200	86.900
1987	9/16/86	578.000	9/24/86	607.800	29.800	116.700
1988	9/16/87	592.100	9/24/87	602.800	10.700	127.400
1989	9/16/88	518.600	9/20/88	497.000	−21.600	105.800
1990	9/18/89	478.200	9/25/89	490.900	12.700	118.500
1991	9/17/90	465.400	9/24/90	467.500	2.100	120.600
1992	9/16/91	354.200	9/24/91	361.400	7.200	127.800
1993	9/16/92	365.400	9/24/92	368.700	3.300	131.100
1994	9/16/93	362.300	9/24/93	365.100	2.800	133.900
1995	9/16/94	417.300	9/26/94	423.200	5.900	139.800
1996	9/18/95	439.500	9/22/95	421.800	−17.700	122.100
1997	9/16/96	391.800	9/24/96	392.000	0.200	122.300

Trades: 25	Average Profit: 11.99
Winners: 19	Average Loss: −17.58
Losers: 6	% Average Profit: 3.26
% Winners: 76.00	% Average Loss: −4.73

Note: There is a risk of loss in futures trading.

TABLE D-9   February Live Hogs
(Enter: 10/30; Exit: 11/29; Stop: 5; P/L Ratio: 3.12)

Year	Date In	Price In	Date Out	Price Out	Profit/Loss	Total
1970	10/30/69	25.350	12/1/69	27.650	2.300	2.300
1971	10/30/70	16.900	11/30/70	16.950	0.050	2.350
1972	11/1/71	22.070	11/29/71	23.520	1.450	3.800
1973	10/30/72	28.700	11/29/72	29.700	1.000	4.800
1974	10/30/73	45.070	11/29/73	46.200	1.130	5.930
1975	10/30/74	42.450	11/29/74	44.300	1.850	7.780
1976	10/30/75	49.900	12/1/75	51.700	1.800	9.580
1977	11/1/76	30.250	11/29/76	30.920	0.670	10.250
1978	10/31/77	36.300	11/29/77	39.100	2.800	13.050
1979	10/30/78	49.950	11/29/78	53.350	3.400	16.450
1980	10/30/79	40.400	11/29/79	42.320	1.920	18.370
1981	10/30/80	55.500	12/1/80	56.800	1.300	19.670
1982	10/30/81	49.820	11/20/81	46.300	−3.520	16.150
1983	11/1/82	53.800	11/29/82	56.850	3.050	19.200
1984	10/31/83	46.950	11/29/83	47.570	0.620	19.820
1985	10/30/84	49.950	11/29/84	53.000	3.050	22.870
1986	10/30/85	45.770	11/29/85	47.650	1.880	24.750
1987	10/30/86	50.400	12/1/86	53.070	2.670	27.420
1988	10/30/87	41.650	11/30/87	42.620	0.970	28.390
1989	10/31/88	45.520	11/18/88	43.100	−2.420	25.970
1990	10/30/89	45.420	11/29/89	49.520	4.100	30.070
1991	10/30/90	49.550	11/29/90	48.100	−1.450	28.620
1992	10/30/91	42.070	11/29/91	42.470	0.400	29.020
1993	10/30/92	42.220	11/30/92	43.370	1.150	30.170
1994	11/1/93	50.070	11/16/93	47.500	−2.570	27.600
1995	10/31/94	37.950	11/16/94	35.120	−2.830	24.770
1996	10/30/95	47.470	11/29/95	47.150	−0.320	24.450
1997	10/30/96	74.950	11/29/96	78.350	3.400	27.850

Trades: 28	Average Profit: 1.86
Winners: 22	Average Loss: −2.19
Losers: 6	% Average Profit: 4.35
% Winners: 78.57	% Average Loss: −4.76

Note: There is a risk of loss in futures trading.

TABLE D-10   Long December Live Hogs
(Enter: 11/9; Exit: 11/23; Stop: 7; P/L Ratio: 3.03)

Year	Date In	Price In	Date Out	Price Out	Profit/Loss	Total
1970	11/9/70	16.450	11/23/70	16.850	0.400	0.400
1971	11/9/71	21.870	11/23/71	22.150	0.280	0.680
1972	11/9/72	29.570	11/27/72	30.300	0.730	1.410
1973	11/9/73	46.200	11/23/73	45.970	−0.230	1.180
1974	11/11/74	39.820	11/25/74	41.120	1.300	2.480
1975	11/10/75	55.320	11/24/75	56.320	1.000	3.480
1976	11/9/76	33.600	11/23/76	34.000	0.400	3.880
1977	11/9/77	38.820	11/23/77	41.950	3.130	7.010
1978	11/9/78	51.400	11/27/78	53.320	1.920	8.930
1979	11/9/79	40.220	11/23/79	42.570	2.350	11.280
1980	11/10/80	50.020	11/24/80	50.170	0.150	11.430
1981	11/9/81	48.150	11/23/81	43.670	−4.480	6.950
1982	11/9/82	54.420	11/23/82	55.720	1.300	8.250
1983	11/9/83	42.350	11/23/83	42.620	0.270	8.520
1984	11/9/84	50.170	11/23/84	53.070	2.900	11.420
1985	11/11/85	47.050	11/25/85	47.200	0.150	11.570
1986	11/10/86	52.700	11/24/86	54.700	2.000	13.570
1987	11/9/87	43.620	11/23/87	44.470	0.850	14.420
1988	11/9/88	40.620	11/23/88	39.900	−0.720	13.700
1989	11/9/89	47.520	11/24/89	51.120	3.600	17.300
1990	11/9/90	52.650	11/23/90	53.450	0.800	18.100
1991	11/11/91	42.550	11/25/91	41.770	−0.780	17.320
1992	11/9/92	43.250	11/23/92	44.570	1.320	18.640
1993	11/9/93	46.570	11/23/93	45.270	−1.300	17.340
1994	11/9/94	32.900	11/23/94	31.650	−1.250	16.090
1995	11/9/95	43.620	11/24/95	44.550	0.930	17.020
1996	11/11/96	57.920	11/25/96	58.670	0.750	17.770

Trades: 27	Average Profit: 1.26
Winners: 21	Average Loss: −1.46
Losers: 6	% Average Profit: 2.90
% Winners: 77.78	% Average Loss: −3.33

Note: There is a risk of loss in futures trading.

TABLE D-11   Short May Oats
(Enter: 12/15; Exit: 2/1; Stop: 8; P/L Ratio: 2.40)

Year	Date In	Price In	Date Out	Price Out	Profit/Loss	Total
1975	12/16/74	176.000	2/3/75	156.250	19.750	19.750
1976	12/15/75	140.000	1/13/76	152.000	−12.000	7.750
1977	12/15/76	163.750	1/26/77	179.500	−15.750	−8.000
1978	12/15/77	135.500	2/1/78	135.000	0.500	−7.500
1979	12/15/78	148.500	2/1/79	143.500	5.000	−2.500
1980	12/17/79	164.500	2/1/80	156.000	8.500	6.000
1981	12/5/80	230.750	2/2/81	212.500	18.250	24.250
1982	12/15/81	183.500	12/31/81	200.250	−16.750	7.500
1983	12/15/82	15.250	2/1/83	174.750	0.500	8.000
1984	12/15/83	184.250	2/1/84	180.500	3.750	11.750
1985	12/17/84	173.750	2/1/85	173.000	0.750	12.500
1986	12/16/85	140.000	2/3/86	123.000	17.000	29.500
1987	12/15/86	152.250	2/2/87	155.000	−2.750	26.750
1988	12/15/87	184.000	2/1/88	183.000	1.000	27.750
1989	12/15/88	227.500	2/1/89	221.000	6.500	34.250
1990	12/15/89	162.750	2/1/90	144.250	18.500	52.750
1991	12/17/90	124.500	2/1/91	115.000	9.500	62.250
1992	12/16/91	139.000	1/30/92	153.000	−14.000	48.250
1993	12/15/92	152.750	2/1/93	141.500	11.250	59.500
1994	12/15/93	140.500	2/1/94	136.500	4.000	63.500
1995	12/15/94	127.000	2/1/95	125.000	2.000	65.500
1996	12/15/95	237.500	2/1/96	226.750	10.750	76.250
1997	12/16/96	160.000	2/3/97	150.750	9.250	85.500

Trades: 23	Average Profit: 8.15
Winners: 18	Average Loss: −12.25
Losers: 5	% Average Profit: 4.86
% Winners: 78.26	% Average Loss: −7.84

Note: There is a risk of loss in futures trading.

APPENDIX E

SOFTWARE USED IN WRITING THIS BOOK

CQG System One and CQG for Windows, registered trademarks of CQG, Inc., P.O. Box 758, Glenwood Springs, CO 81602, 800-525-7082, were used to generate the charts so credited in the figure captions.

Microsoft Excel was used to generate the monthly cash market analysis data. Microsoft Excel is a registered trademark of Microsoft Corporation, One Microsoft Way, Redmond, WA 98052-6399, 206-635-7070.

Omega TradeStation software was used to confirm the futures data. Figures 7-1 and 7-2 were created with SuperCharts. Omega TradeStation and SuperCharts are registered trademark of Omega Research, Inc., 8700 West Flagler Street, Suite 250, Miami, FL 33174-2428, 800-556-2022.

Host software was used to generate the key date seasonal trades. Host is a registered trademark of MBH Commodity Advisors, Inc., P.O. Box 353, Winnetka, IL 60093, 847-291-1870.

INDEX